THANK YOU

for purchasing
The Moon Apothecary

Scan here to gain access to
exclusive bonus content.

xoxo, Lorriane ♡

THE MOON

APOTHECARY

Rituals and Recipes for the Lunar Phases

LORRIANE ANDERSON

ROCKPOOL

A Rockpool book
PO Box 252
Summer Hill
NSW 2130
Australia

rockpoolpublishing.com
Follow us! **f** **⊙** rockpoolpublishing
Tag your images with #rockpoolpublishing

ISBN: 9781925946802

Published in 2024 by Rockpool Publishing

Design and typesetting by Sara Lindberg, Rockpool Publishing
Edited by Lisa Macken
Images from Shutterstock

A catalogue record for this
book is available from the
National Library of Australia

The information in this book is not intended as medical advice. Readers are recommended to
consult a qualified medical specialist for individual advice. The author, editors and publisher
of this work cannot be held liable for any errors or omissions, or actions that may be taken as a
consequence of the information contained in this work.

A note about the recipes
This book uses US cup and spoon measures.
1 teaspoon = 5 ml
1 tablespoon = 15 ml
1 cup = approx. 240 ml

Printed and bound in China
10 9 8 7 6 5 4 3 2 1

CONTENTS

INTRODUCTION

Hello, darling. My name is Lorriane and I am in love with spiritual wellness, seasonal self-care, and mindful living. I don't know that there's any one thing that's unleashed this spiritual journey of mine, but there are some staple practices and tools that have sustained me through the good, bad, completely disastrous, and absolutely miraculous cycles of my life. One of these foundational practices for me is working with moon energy.

I started working with the moon almost 10 years ago and I continue to seek out luna for guidance and a deeper understanding of myself today. I had completely turned my back on spirituality for about a year when I started my first spiritual brand. I was unfulfilled and couldn't seem to get any traction, then one day I felt inspired to break out my watercolors. After sitting at a blank page for an hour I felt called to paint the moon phases.

Suddenly, the idea of a moon-based apothecary popped into my brain. Instead of moon phases I called it Moon Phace to represent beauty – the face – combined with the phases of the moon. I didn't tell a soul about my plans but quietly started an Instagram page, began promoting, and spent the last $100 I had to my name to buy enough supplies to make one of each product. I promoted for exactly one month prior to my release, and to my surprise I had orders the very first day and have had consistent growth ever since.

I decided to take a deeper dive into this intuitive ping of moon energy and went from being anti-spiritual to fully immersed in cosmic self-care. My entire life shifted in ways I couldn't have imagined. Following that one little intuitive download has unlocked the door to years and years of personal and spiritual growth as well as evolving success. You probably wouldn't even be holding this book in your hands right now if I had dismissed that small urge to follow the moon.

I truly believe success and self-care go hand in hand. The more you take care of both your physical and spiritual bodies, the more your higher self will support you on the material plane. Since my teens I have spent a great deal of time and effort on beauty and wellness care. For a long time, that was the only thing I truly loved to do until spirituality entered my life and I found myself with the same level of love for spiritual well-being. Ultimately, I found a way to mash my two great loves together.

That is my offering to you in this book: a collection of moon-based spiritual self-care, beauty, and wellness recipes to invite both spiritual and physical nourishment into your life. The information contained in this book is the embodiment of years of trial and error, research, and spiritual guidance. There's no shortage of moon-based products for purchase these days, but they do not take into consideration your personal energy, goals, and needs.

In this book you will use the intelligence of the moon phases to discover your deepest desires and learn how you can channel your intentions into everyday self-care such as lotions and creams, oils and sprays, comforting teas, cleansing soaps, ritual baths and more. You will be armed with the knowledge to create a new beauty potion for every single moon phase or transit through a new sign, if that is what you desire.

In addition to the moon phases – new, waxing crescent, first quarter, waxing gibbous, full, waning gibbous, last quarter and waning crescent – you will also find knowledge and inspiration for creating potions based on the zodiac signs as they apply to the moon, and special moon events such as blue moons and the eclipses. As you flow through the pages of this book, remember that:

- No one knows you and your energy like you do. If something doesn't feel right, move on to something that is more aligned with what brings you comfort and joy.

- There is no right or wrong way to practice your spirituality. The information in this book is based on my experience and serves as a guideline, not a rule book. Take liberties to adapt, add, or release anything from my recipes that do not serve your ultimate goals.

- Talking to the moon is not crazy unless you decide that it is.

- Working with the full breadth of moon cycles can be overwhelming at first. It's perfectly fine to start slow and add more as you go along.

PART I

MOON MAGIC MAKER

CHAPTER 1

MAGIC
AND
RESPONSIBILITY

SAFETY FIRST

Potion making is a fun and rewarding process, but there are a few housekeeping rules to keep in mind before jumping in. Most of the ingredients you will use are considered safe when handled properly. However, it's important to always consult with a doctor or other qualified professional if you are unsure how an ingredient will affect you and **always** if you are pregnant, nursing, or suffering from any disease or illness.

CONNECTING WITH THE SPIRIT OF INGREDIENTS

My gateway to spirituality has always been plants. I love their texture and smell, and the overall sensual experience of delighting in the thousands of ways Mother Earth expresses herself. Over the years, I have learned everything I could about deepening my connection with the material I use to craft my potions. I've learned the value of plant dreaming and companionship, animism – the practice of acknowledging the soul present within non-human beings – and honoring the intelligence of earth material shaped over millions of years. Millions of plant species, crystals, animals, and minerals existed on this planet for millennia before humans did. They have so much to share and teach when you learn to slow down and listen to their offerings.

Approach your ingredients with reverence. The respect you show to the materials used will be repaid in the effectiveness of your potions. I often talk to my herbs and essential oils before working with them, asking them to share with me their wisdom. I pledge to use their guidance in the way it was intended. They'll often say, "Yes, Lorriane, I'll be perfect in this cream," or "No, Lorriane, I'm not right for this perfume." For a long time I dismissed these conversations as silly or things I'd made up, but with time I came to trust in the intuitive pings I received from my ingredients and so will you.

Now I listen and I honor the wisdom of Mother Earth. I take time to get to know my ingredients, asking them to tell me about their home land or to understand what was involved in their journey to my apothecary. It isn't common to believe herbs have a soul, but they are living, breathing creatures just like you and me that have given their lives and been taken away from the vitality of other species for the benefit of your desires. Crystals were displaced from their earthen homes to join you on your spiritual quest. Repay their gift to you by taking the time to understand how they came to be with you and showing them the respect they are rightfully owed.

Research the native environment in which your plants grow, as knowing how they behave will provide a lot of information about their spiritual benefits and intelligence. Find out if your material is organic or sustainably harvested or on the brink of extinction before selecting it as a component in your formulations, and grow as much of it as you can. Nurturing and caring for your materials create an unmistakable bond, not unlike that between parent to child.

Dream with your ingredients. Sleep with them. Drink them if you can and speak to them. Get to know your material in as much detail as possible, all the while tuning in to their magic. Your time with them will provide more information than anything in any book or on any blog. You will develop a deeper understanding of what it means to see the soul and magic in everything.

CULTURAL MINDFULNESS

Cultural appropriation is a big topic these days and rightfully so: for years, it was considered okay to steal and exploit practices from other cultures without permission. As a black person of color, I have watched the appropriation of black culture again and again and again. A perfect example of cultural appropriation are zombies, a pop-culture phenomenon stolen from voodoo. Of course, cultural appropriation extends far beyond black culture into nearly every culture in the world. The popular spiritual practice of smudging originated with Native Americans. The concept of smoke clearing isn't specific to Native Americans but the use of white sage for this purpose and the specific term "smudging" are, and smudging has become so popular that white sage is now endangered.

I believe it is okay to appreciate a culture that is not your own and be inspired by it, but to steal it without permission or credit, use it without a clear understanding of its meaning and origins, or exploit it for financial gain are some ways appreciation becomes appropriation. I have been guilty of such behavior and I am actively trying to do my part as a person of color, and a person in general, to be mindful of how I'm contributing to the problem. I still have work to do, of course, but every day I learn a new way to be more responsible in my approach to spiritual workings.

On the opposite end of the spectrum is listening to your ancestral DNA. Advancements in DNA research allow us to discover our heritage with simple and mostly inexpensive at-home tests. Though on the outside I am a black woman my DNA is fairly complex, with nearly one-third of my DNA being of European and Asian descent. The remaining part of my DNA consists of various African regions, and knowing this information has allowed me to connect with spiritual practices I didn't even know existed or were available to me. I've been able to add new layers of intention and understanding, based completely on knowing what's flowing through my veins.

My heritage studies have led me to the Yoruba people and voodoo cultures of West Africa, as well as opened the door to learning more about my Scandinavian and British heritages. What's interesting is that I have come to realize the cultures I have always felt drawn to are ones that ended up in my DNA profile. I don't believe in coincidence, but I do believe I was led to these cultures because my soul is already familiar with them through my ancestral ties. If you haven't already, I encourage you to find out your DNA story and how it relates to the development of your spiritual practice.

That said, having DNA is not the same thing as having a lived experience. While one-third of my heritage is European, I also acknowledge I have not had a European lived experience – meaning I did not grow up with the customs and cultures that are specific to these groups of people. I greatly enjoy learning about my heritage but I still approach new practices with humility, and I often remind myself that, while I am connected to many cultures through my DNA, it is not my right to use or misuse things I do not understand. There's a part of my spirit that intuitively knows what to do, but I accept that there's always more to learn.

SUSTAINABILITY

Herbalism and aromatherapy have quickly become popular, mainstream interests. The herbalism industry is estimated to be in the billions of dollars per year. As a result, many plants and herbs are at risk and we should be mindful when selecting them for spiritual workings. I suspect this trend will continue over the coming years as spirituality, herbalism, and alternative medicines in general become more popular. If possible, grow as much of your herbs as you can, only purchase from sources that practice sustainable harvesting methods, and look for alternatives to any of the herbs featured on the list of at-risk plants opposite. There are often multiple options to represent a specific intention without needing to use an at-risk herb. Keep in mind that the status of plants is an evolving matter and this list may grow over time.

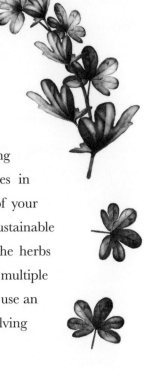

- American ginseng (*Panax quinquefolius*)
- black cohosh (*Actaea racemosa, Cimicifuga racemosa*)
- bloodroot (*Sanguinaria canadensis*)
- blue cohosh (*Caulophyllum thalictroides*)
- echinacea (*Echinacea* spp.)
- eyebright (*Euphrasia* spp.)
- goldenseal (*Hydrastis canadensis*)
- helonias root (*Chamaelirium luteum*)
- kava kava (*Piper methysticum*), Hawaii only
- lady's slipper (*Cypripedium* spp.)
- lomatium (*Lomatium dissectum*)
- osha (*Ligusticum porteri, L.* spp.)
- peyote (*Lophophora williamsii*)
- slippery elm (*Ulmus rubra*)
- sundew (*Drosera* spp.)
- trillium, beth root (*Trillium* spp.)
- true unicorn (*Aletris farinosa*)
- venus fly trap (*Dionaea muscipula*)
- Virginia snakeroot (*Aristolochia serpentaria*)
- wild yam (*Dioscorea villosa, D.* spp.).

CHAPTER 2

THE MOON APOTHECARY

PLANTS

An apothecary isn't complete without plants, flowers, and herbs. Plant material is widely accessible online and more unique herbs can now be found in major health food stores, with more becoming available every day. They can be purchased dried, in powdered form and, in some cases, fresh. And if you have a green thumb, I highly suggest purchasing seeds and starting your own moon garden.

Powdered herbs are lovely in bath salts, scrubs, face masks and exfoliants, or incense. Whole dried herbs are used to make tinctures and infused oils but can also be used for steams, loose incense, offerings, and as teas. Fresh herbs can be

dried and powdered or used to make single use preparations, teas, and foods. There are hundreds, if not thousands, of herbs to choose from but I have narrowed down a list of plants for each moon phase, which you can find at the beginning of each moon chapter in Part II.

FRAGRANCE OILS

Fortunately, fragrance oils have come a long way over the years and there is now a wide variety of sources offering clean fragrances. Whether or not you use fragrance oils is a personal choice, but in terms of spiritual work fragrance oils do not carry any discernible energy. There is no way to know what's in a fragrance oil and, therefore, you could be introducing a low-vibrational component to your blend.

Fragrance oils can, however, open up your potions to a wider perfumed experience that essential oils cannot provide alone. For a long time I'd only work with essential oils but, sadly, the huge demand for herbs and essential oils have put a strain on availability and sustainability, so I am much more mindful these days to seek other options that aren't as taxing to the earth.

I also really love fragrances of all kinds and find myself being drawn to them a lot more now that there are much safer options to choose from. If you do decide to use fragrance oils, take steps to protect your energy by clearing the bottles when they arrive and then properly clearing and dedicating the potion once it's made.

There are also plant-based fragrance oils that do carry specific vibrational intentions based on the individual components. When using plant-based fragrance oils, be sure to only purchase from a reputable company that is transparent about the ingredients used to create the blend. That way, you'll have an understanding of the energetic frequency and can make an informed choice when deciding to use it.

ESSENTIAL OILS

An essential oil blend doesn't have to smell herbaceous or earthy to be effective. With a little bit of perfumery knowledge, you can make blends that are potent but also pleasing to your nose. The key is in figuring out which scents resonate with you. I'm pretty partial to woods, heartier florals such as neroli and lavender, and citrus notes such as bergamot and tangerine. I use these essential oils a lot because I connect with them the most and they provide me with the best scent experience. And because I love the smell, it's easier to connect with my potion's energy during ritual and spellwork.

There are a few ways to go about creating a scent blend, which you'll learn about in Chapter 4. Below are a few things to keep in mind when working with essential oils. These little oils are magical but can cause significant irritation when used incorrectly. I do not advise taking essential oils internally under any circumstances, despite some online information suggesting otherwise. Essential oils are highly concentrated, and though they come from plants essential oils are indeed chemical compounds. Taking the oils internally can lead to allergic reactions, interfere with medications, and may contribute to negative long-term effects.

When using them externally, it's important to dilute them properly before applying to the skin, especially when used in a bath. Water disperses essential oils, and from my experience a few drops of undiluted essential oil, even one or two, can cause skin irritations and even burning. For the recipes in this book, generally 20 to 50 drops is enough for a 2 oz | 60 ml potion.

Essential Oils to Avoid During Pregnancy

The use of essential oils during pregnancy is a sensitive topic. There are some who swear by certain essential oils for pregnancy and some people who believe you should avoid all of them until birth. It's very common for women to develop sensitivity to essential oils during pregnancy, even if you've used them for a long time. Stop using any essential oils immediately if they cause discomfort, and be sure to check with your doctor if you have any concerns about their safety. Below is a list of essential oils that are generally considered unsafe for pregnancy because they can cause contractions or other complications:

Aniseed	Cedarwood/thuja	Hyssop	Parsley	Tansy
Basil	Cinnamon	Juniper berry	Pennyroyal	Tarragon
Birch	Clary sage	Marjoram	Rosemary	Tonka
Camphor	Clove	Mugwort	Ruse	Wintergreen
Caraway	Deertongue	Nutmeg	Sage	Wormwood
Cassia	Fennel	Oregano	Sassafras	

Inauthentic Essential Oils

There are some fragrances that are lovely but either do not exist in essential oil form, are incredibly expensive, or are not readily available to the public. I can't tell you how many times someone has asked me to create a product using oud essential oil, one of the rarest and most expensive oils in the world. Oud, also known as agarwood, can cost $1,000 per ounce or more, wholesale. If ever you come across a product that claims to be fragranced with oud or agarwood and it doesn't cost hundreds of dollars, chances of there being any real oud in the contents are slim to none. It's more likely to be a fragrance oil.

Below is a list of oils that may be inauthentic to keep in mind when shopping for ingredients. Take caution when purchasing these oils and do research on the company before purchasing from them, especially if the price seems too good to be true. All of these plants have spiritual properties; however, they all share properties with other plant materials that are less expensive and easier to find from reputable sources:

- Lily of the valley: There is said to be an absolute, but I have not found a reputable source for such a product.

- Honeysuckle: Very expensive but it is available.

- Oud: Arguably the most expensive essential oil in the world and costs more than $1,000 per ounce. It is almost always synthetic and nearly impossible to find.

- Lotus: Lotus absolute is very difficult to find, and when you do it is very costly. Blue, white, or pink lotus generally ranges from $90 to $200 per ounce wholesale, and is not readily available as it is produced nearly exclusively in India and only during specific seasons.

- Coconut: Coconut oil is a fatty, vegetable oil. Virgin coconut does have some scent but can vary in degree of fragrance. Coconut essential oil does not exist, and any fragrance claiming to contain such is synthetic or an extract. You can use coconut extract in water-based formulas.

- Honey essential oil: This is actually beeswax absolute. Copaiba balsam is often sold as honey essential oil as it is sometimes called honey balsam, which comes from a tree native to Brazil and not from bees.

- Carnation: This is very expensive.

- Gardenia: Exists both in essential oil and absolute form; however, it is very costly and caution should be exercised if the cost is low. Gardenia absolute generally starts around $90 per ounce. Gardenia essential oil is very rare and almost always synthetic.

- Berries: Raspberry, strawberry, blackberry, and blueberry are all synthetic, as these fruits do not produce essential oil. Their seeds, however, can produce oil and would be considered carrier oils (see below). They have little to no scent.

- Violet: Violet is very expensive but it is available.

EXTRACTS

Extracts are generally alcohol based and can offer some fragrance in water-based formulas; however, they are most useful for introducing the energy of a plant that is either not readily available or too costly in essential oil form.

Many extracts are not oil soluble, which means they will not mix with the oil in your formulation. Most are water soluble and will dissolve completely into waters or liquids. Extracts are ideal when you'd like to infuse the energy of a plant that is only available as a vegetable oil such as coconut, pecan, or pomegranate, or for essential oils that are very costly such as vanilla absolute. You can find a wide variety of extracts in specialty food stores or online. Avoid imitation extracts, which are made with chemical components, animal components, or other unknown materials.

CARRIER OILS

Carrier oils are sometimes called base, fixed, or vegetable oils. They are created from a variety of plant materials such as nuts, seeds, fruits, and vegetables, as the name suggests. Just as with essential oils, each carrier oil has a unique energetic frequency that can enhance or dilute the energy of your blends. Sadly, they are often overlooked in spiritual formulations. Essential oils and herbs are perhaps the most important parts of your magical creations, but I find carrier oils play a significant role as well. Over recent years, I have experimented both in my personal practice and with the products I craft for my spiritual apothecary Spirit Element, adding carrier oils to my body and ritual oils and other products where a vegetable oil is appropriate. I've found my magical blends to be much more sophisticated and effective, both from practical and spiritual perspectives. Keeping the spiritual properties of carrier oils in mind when making your blends will give you an opportunity to add one more layer of magic and intent. You will find the carrier oils that best support each moon phase in the moon chapters in Part II.

CREAMS AND LOTIONS

Creams and lotions are a great, everyday way to take advantage of a magical blend. Creams and lotions can easily be customized to fit your spiritual needs, but there's only so many ways to add layers to your creams if you're purchasing them commercially. Creams and lotions are easy to make at home with a little bit of practice, and you'll be able to customize every aspect of your blend. Lotions and creams are made the same way, the difference being the amount of water or oil/wax used. A lotion has more water than oil and is lightweight because of the high water content. A cream has more oil than water and is ideal for very dry skin that tends to lose moisture easily. The high oil content locks water in skin, allowing you to maintain moisture for longer periods of time.

You can customize your cream mixtures by using different kinds of floral waters or different oils. Keep in mind that each ingredient has skin properties too, and you'll want to take this into consideration. For example, olive oil is great for wealth but is also a very thick oil. If you have oily skin, you may want to consider a lighter oil such as grapeseed – an excellent all-purpose option. The same goes for hydrosols and floral waters. Peppermint would be wonderful in a lotion for daily spiritual cleansing for someone with acne-prone skin but may be too drying for dry skin. Geranium, on the other hand, is another excellent choice for daily spiritual cleansing but is much more suitable for dry skin needs.

SALTS AND SUGARS

Salts and sugars are the perfect base for body and hair scrubs and, like plants and oils, each one has a specific property that lends itself to your moon-minded potions. Salts in general are spiritually cleansing and best suited for the waning moon phases. Sugars, on the other hand, correspond to love, sex, feminine energies, and sweetness. I consider sugar to be more of a waxing and full moon ingredient. You'll likely find black salts being used for the new moon and white salt or sugar for the full moon, but don't feel limited to just those. While there is no right or wrong time to use any of these salts and sugars, I have found some personal correspondence for each item listed below:

- White salt: All phases, full moon phase.
- Black salt: Waning and new moon phases.
- Pink salt: Waxing gibbous and full moon phases.
- Gray salt: Waning and new moon phases.
- Red salt: First quarter phase.
- White sugar: All phases, full moon phase.
- Brown sugar: Waxing phases.
- Coconut sugar: Last quarter and last crescent phases.
- Raw sugar or sugar cane: Waxing phases.

CLAYS

Individual clays do not have specific metaphysical properties, but clays overall do correspond to the earth and are amazing in beauty magic for use on the face and hair. Different clays have different minerals, creating their unique color profile. Add them based on their use for the skin first, then consider the color as it relates to your intention. Here are some frequently used clays:

- Bentonite: One of the most common and widely available clays on the market, bentonite is used in everything from tooth powders to cleansing hair and, of course, face masks. It is an all-purpose option that is suitable for nearly every skin type.

- French green clay: Otherwise known simply as 'green clay', French green clay is best suited to problematic and oily skin. It can be a bit harsh, and those with sensitive skin should avoid it. Of all the clays, this one aligns the most with the earth element and grounding. I like to use it for the last quarter moon.

- White clay: This is the mildest of all the clays and is commonly known as 'cosmetic clay'. It is most suitable for very dry, sensitive or mature skin. Because white symbolizes purity, I like to add it to recipes for connecting with spiritual wisdom, clarity, and light energy. Try this one at a full moon.

- Red clay: This clay is a beautiful, rusty brick color but, be mindful, as it can stain. It's best to use it in small amounts and mixed in with other clays or plant materials. Red clay is most suited to dry to normal skin and is relatively mild.

- Activated charcoal: This is not actually a clay but it is great for problematic skin. It attaches to and draws out toxins and impurities, and is ideal for all skin types. Charcoal can also be used internally to draw out toxins, but should be taken within four hours of medication. Charcoal can also be added to salts to create black salt for ritual purposes.

WATER

Distilled water should be used for any preparations intended for the body that call for water such as toners, teas, sprays, room sprays, and herbal infusions. Distilled water is created by boiling it into vapor, then condensing it back into liquid form. Doing so removes impurities and bacteria that could introduce mold and other harmful contaminants into your potions. Distilled water is easy to find in all major grocery stores. It's okay to use other sources of water for altar, room or ritual sprays. Some ideas include water from:

- rain
- melted snow
- inside a successful business
- rivers, lakes, or the ocean
- a place that holds special meaning.

If your potion is a body formulation and requires water from an unpurified source, simply boil the water and cool it before adding it to your blend. You may also want to add a tablespoon or two of high-proof alcohol to reduce the risk of bacterial growth.

Hydrosols and Floral Waters

Herbal distillates, more commonly known as hydrosols and floral waters, can be used in place of or in addition to distilled water. The most common and readily available ones are rosewater, lavender water, and orange blossom, but a hydrosol can be made with nearly any plant material. Some of my favorites are jasmine, vetiver, cucumber, baked earth, and cypress, but you can find a wide variety of options online.

Hydrosols and floral waters are also distilled, therefore any contaminants have been removed and are safe for use in body formulations. They contain small amounts of essential oil – usually 1 percent or less – from the plant material used to create them, giving them the added attraction of spiritual and medicinal benefits. Though the amount of essential oil is small, you will find most hydrosols and floral waters are quite fragrant and can add an extra layer to both your potion's magic and the scent experience. Be sure to purchase them from a reputable source, as many commercialized hydrosols are actually distilled water with drops of essential or fragrance oil.

Keep hydrosols and floral waters in dark containers and in the refrigerator if possible or out of direct sunlight. Herbal distillates are highly volatile and can spoil very quickly, and each one spoils at different rates. With proper care, most hydrosols and floral waters will last six to eight months. Throw away the water if it comes cloudy, develops a smell, or sediment begins to form.

Moon Water

You can add an extra layer of magic to your water, hydrosols, or floral waters by charging them. The most common way to charge water is by placing them in direct sunlight or moonlight for several hours. The waters will absorb the energy of the sun or moon and carry their spiritual properties into your potions. Some additional ways to charge waters include:

- based on the current sun or moon sign
- during a specific celestial event such as a lunar eclipse
- placing them on an altar
- placing them on top of a photo or symbol, or tapping it against the container
- infusing them with crystals.

To charge your water, fill a glass jar with distilled or boiled water. Place it outside or on a windowsill on the day or night that corresponds with your desired energetic intention. Allow it to "charge" for at least six hours. Store the jar away from sunlight and use it as needed. Add the charged water to your formulations, bath spells, floor washes, and aromatherapy diffuser.

ALCOHOLS AND WITCH HAZEL

I love adding alcohol to my sprays. Each one has a unique scent profile that can really enhance the other ingredients. Whiskey pairs well with woods and vanilla, brandy with sweeter fragrances and florals, vodka is perfect for fresh and bright blends, and gin is excellent for juniper, of course. Not only do they add complexity to your fragrance, but they serve a practical use as well. Alcohol helps to prevent bacterial growth and can extend the shelf life of your formulas, and can also be infused with plant material that is not readily available in essential oil form – adding one more layer of intention and magic. Try infusing alcohol with unusual ingredients such as moss, fruits, vegetables, vanilla beans, or dragon's blood resin, as I've done in the Releasing Body Scrub recipe on page 164.

Commercially prepared witch hazel can also be used to add an astringent quality to water based formulas. It isn't as powerful as alcohol for reducing bacteria but makes a gentle toner for beauty magic. You can also create a witch hazel tincture by infusing witch hazel bark into alcohol though unlike the commercial version, a witch hazel tincture will create a brown like liquid and take on the smell of the alcohol used.

CRYSTALS

I love adding crystals to my formulations, especially when I'm making a product that is exclusively used for ritual purposes. However, crystals should be used sparingly in formulations that are going to be applied to the skin. Many crystals are toxic when ingested, and the same goes for a crystal that has been sitting in a body oil, cream, or any formulation with a liquid/oil component. Some crystals contain metals and can rust in water. Therefore, caution should be exercised when adding a crystal to your next potion.

You can take more liberties when making formulations that are not made for the skin. For example, an anointing oil for enhanced psychic abilities that is only used for dressing candles is an excellent product to infuse with a crystal such as lapis that wouldn't normally be safe for skin use. A ritual spray used to clear your space before beginning ceremonial work could be amplified with rutilated quartz to raise vibrations, or if you've made a floor wash to protect your home you may want to toss a piece of black tourmaline in the bucket as you mop.

As always, you should do your own research to make sure you are comfortable with your ingredients. Below is a list of crystals and their properties that I use regularly in skincare formulations and are included in my beloved crystal bath bars, which you can find on my store's website:

- Quartz: Use in place of moonstone when a water-safe crystal is needed. Clear quartz can be programmed for any intention, making it an excellent all-purpose stone. It also amplifies energy and unblocks stagnant energy. It can be used for both the waxing and waning moon phases.

- Amethyst: Use in place of intuition crystals such as labradorite or lapis when a water-safe crystal is needed. This stone works well with both the waxing and waning phases of the moon. Use it during the waxing phases for creativity and unlocking psychic gifts and during the waning phases for stress relief, overcoming mood swings, and supporting emotional well-being.

- Citrine: An excellent stone for work during the waxing phases of the moon, but especially the waning crescent and first quarter moons. Use it in blends for self-expression, manifestation, acquiring wealth, and promoting happiness.

- Smoky quartz: A powerful stone for protection and clearing low vibrations. It is best suited for the waning phases of the moon but is also supportive during the dark or new moon phases. Use it to clear stagnant and low vibrations, overcoming intense emotions, and grounding.

- Red jasper: A personal favorite for grounding meditation; however, red jasper is a lovely all-purpose stone for all phases of the moon. It promotes passion and stamina, making it an excellent choice during the waxing moon if you are lacking motivation. It also clears and restores the aura, providing additional self-care during the waning phases. Its balancing properties align with full and new moons.

- Petrified wood: This is not actually a crystal but minerally preserved wood, bringing a clear connection to earth energies and grounding. It is a stone of slow transformation and is ideal to work with for long periods of time. Consider working with petrified wood for an entire moon cycle to deal with any struggles to adapt to change and to learn to be present in each phase.

CHAPTER 3

SYNERGY

LAYERS OF INTENTION

The art of making spiritually based beauty and wellness formulations lies in correspondences or what I prefer to call "layers of intention." Everything is energy, including the materials used to make your potions, and has a vibrational signature that represents an intention such as love, peace, motivation, focus, and so on. Your final formulation also has a personal energy sequence that is determined by the sum of the ingredients you choose to add. Each layer of intention adds to the quality of your potion's energetic frequency.

Jasmine as an oil or flower is most aligned with moon energy and is perfectly wonderful all on its own. Jasmine primarily represents beauty, night and moon energy, enhanced divination, and emotional healing, all of which are excellent for a potion representing the full moon – but what if you wish to make a waxing moon oil that supports action and confidence? Jasmine might make a fantastic base to represent the moon but your potion could be more energetically effective if you were to add stimulating and motivating ingredients such as ginger or honeysuckle.

You may also wish to have a more complex fragrance experience than jasmine by itself. Personally, I enjoy woodsy scents that are paired with florals and resins but I am mindful that every ingredient used changes the frequency of my final product, so I'll specifically look for wood, floral, and resin notes that support my desired intention. Nearly every component of your potion will have some sort of vibration. Color, fragrance, plant materials, crystals, salts, different kinds of liquids, and even the things you write on the bottle can all support your desired outcome with a little bit of mindfulness and intention.

Be mindful of layering too many intentions, as doing so can create confusion and dilute the effectiveness of your potion. Stay within two to three related intentions so that your creation remains focused and clear, otherwise, your soul won't have an understanding of where to focus its attention and neither will the spirits, deities, or otherworldly beings who have been assigned to assist you.

ABSTRACT INTENTIONS

Some intentions are obvious, such as abundance, peace, or love. Other intentions are a bit more abstract, such as a product based on a lunar eclipse or a full moon in Gemini. Treat these intentions like you would a goal – by breaking them down into smaller, more familiar intentions. The waning moon phases, for example, are associated with reflection, rest, gratitude, awareness, and self-care. You could choose one or two of these smaller intentions to begin to tell the story of your final potion. A bath salt for promoting self-care could encompass the energy of rest and renewal, but it could also represent awareness and gratitude.

If an intention feels too abstract, take a moment to go deeper and ask yourself what this intention means to you? What does self-care or gratitude mean for you? What does it mean to work with the full moon in Scorpio or the new moon in Aquarius? Then, make a list of the feelings or intentions that came up for you during this reflection, and from there pick two or three minor intentions to focus on to begin to tell the story of your potion.

See Bonus Material, page 265, to access the abstract intention worksheet.

COLOR MAGIC

Known as "color theory" in the mainstream, color magic is a widely respected form of psychological influence that is used by billion-dollar corporations as readily as by your neighborhood witch. In spirituality, you'll typically see color magic related to candles but you don't have to stop there. Each color corresponds to a number of energetic themes and can add yet another layer of magic and intention to your formulations.

Many herbs and flowers are available in a variety of colors, and can either change the entire color of your blend or add a pop of interest in addition to the plant's spiritual properties. Tinctures especially take on the color of many plants and can completely change the look of your ritual sprays. Elderberries, for example, create a beautiful deep blue or purple shade. Nettle and comfrey make a striking green, St. John's wort turns a vibrant red, and chamomile introduces a brilliant yellow.

There are also several essential oils that can gently influence your potions look. Tansy and blue chamomile are well known for their royal blue–like hue, whereas many citrus essential oils range from bright yellow to orange. Pink grapefruit specifically has a strong orange hue and easily gives color oils and sprays alike.

There are many options to welcome color into your formulations that are natural and synthetic. Some options are outlined below.

Mica: Mica is a natural, environmentally friendly color pigment sourced from the mineral of the same name and is available in a variety of colors. Look for ethically sourced mica that does not support child labor and is fair trade. To use mica in oil-based formulas, mix with essential oils first, blend into a carrier oil and use as desired. The mica will eventually settle to the bottom, so shake well to reactivate the color magic. To use in water-based formulas, mix well with vegetable glycerin first and then mix into water. Note, however, that some micas mix with water better than others. Experiment with different colors to see which ones create your desired aesthetic.

Plant dyes and powders: There are many powdered plant dyes available that are commonly used in soap production. Powders work best in dry formulas or creations with a low moisture content such as bath salts, soaps, bath bombs, body scrubs, or incense. They can also be used to make botanical ink for writing. They do not mix well with oils and can mold when added to water.

Food coloring: This is a food-grade color option that mixes well with most water-based formulas.

Liquid dyes: There are liquid dyes that are made specifically for the cosmetic industry, but they usually contain harsh chemicals. They are commonly used in makeup pigments for the lips and eyes.

Color Magic Correspondences

There is always the option of experimenting and letting the ingredients show their magic. Play around and see what colors you can create either as individual plant pigments or by combining various plant materials to create new shades.

- Pink: Affection, beauty, children, compassion, domestic harmony, emotional healing, femininity, fidelity, friendship, kindness, love, marriage, nurturing, partnership, romance, self-love.

- Red: Action, ancestral work, assertiveness, blood magic, courage, danger, desire, energy, fire element, independence, overcoming obstacles, passion, power, sexual potency, strength, survival, taking risks, vitality.

- Green: Abundance, acceptance, earth element, expansion, fertility, growth, harmony, healing, intention setting, longevity, luck, money, prosperity, tree and herb magic.

- Blue: Communication, dreams, fidelity, focus, forgiveness, intuition, patience, peace, relaxation, sea magic, sincerity, sleep, spirituality, storm magic, tranquility, truth, water element, wisdom.

- Silver: Awareness, divination, dreams, feminine energy, meditation, moon energy, psychic powers, purification, stability, star magic, success, the goddess.

- Gold: Abundance, ambition, attraction, confidence, fame, happiness, influence, luxury, masculine energy, money, optimism, self-worth, solar magic, success, the god.

- Black: Banishment, binding, clearing negativity, cuttings cords, defense, endings, grief, karma, magick, persistence, protection, release, safety, scrying, shadow work, strength, uncrossing, unhexing, wisdom.

- White: Angel magic, balance, clarity, cleansing, divinity, high vibrations, higher self, hope, innocence, intentions, peace, purity, spiritual guidance and spirit guides, spirituality, the aura, unity, will power. *Note:* When in doubt, go with white. It can be used as an all-purpose candle to hold space for any intention.

- Yellow: Charm, confidence, flexibility, friendship, gut instinct, happiness, inspiration, learning new skills, persuasion, pleasure, solar magic, success, travel.

- Orange: Celebration, confidence, creativity, fertility, freedom, fun, goals, independence, joy, movement, passion for life, positivity, self-acceptance, self-expression, sensuality, stimulation, vitality, womb wisdom.

- Purple: Addiction, air element, akashic records, astrology, authority, enlightenment, imagination, influence, power, psychic protection, self-development, spiritual development, spiritual power, spiritual realms, wisdom.

- Brown: Ancestral work, animal energy, construction, earth magick/element, endurance, financial crisis, grounding, hard work, stability.

COMPOSITION AND ESTHETIC

Another unexpected way to weave in some extra magic is by being mindful of the overall composition. Colors can be layered to create a desired effect, such as a rainbow, or made to resemble a sunset. I once made a bath salt by layering different shades of oranges, yellows, and blue to represent the sunrise. This blend was intended to be used on Saturday mornings to uplift my spirit and encourage joy. During my childhood, it was common for my household to wake up around 5 am, so I rarely missed a sunrise. Now, enjoying a sunrise gives me joy and a feeling of vitality. Having sunrises symbolized in my formulation for happiness added a little extra detail and made it even more special, nostalgic and personalized.

Experiment with different ways to give your spiritual blend an extra flare. Add crystals, herbs, and flowers, layering them, mixing them, and playing around with the overall look and feel. For grounding or earth magic products I like to add smoky quartz to the bottle to represent dirt or mud, then I'll slip in cedar leaf or pine needles to look like trees. For water and sea magic, you'll often find a seashell or two inside the bottle. I also like to add mother of pearl chips and abalone shell pieces, just to represent water energy. For money oils, I sometimes add gold mica flakes to represent wealth or split a formula into black and white to create a salt and pepper effect, representing balance.

CHAPTER 4

CREATING YOUR OWN MOON POTIONS

· · · · · · ·)·)·⟩·◐·❋·☾·☀·☽·⟨·(·(·(· · · · · · ·

The main function of spirit potions and therefore moon potions by extension is to manifest your goals and intentions, whether that's to make more money, cultivate more self-love, or just to have a beautiful cozy day at home. And while there are thousands of beautiful creators out in the world, making every kind of moon potion you can imagine, none of them are you and nor do they have an intimate understanding of your personal goals and desires. You are a beautifully complex person whose goals might change from one moon to the next, and making your own moon potions allows you the freedom to customize your ritual formulations to fit your immediate needs.

In this chapter I outline my current process for making beautiful moon-inspired spirit potions, focusing on invoking your senses to create a unique experience every time you formulate something new. By the end of this chapter you will know how to clearly identify your intentions, create aromas that are not only beautiful but represent your desired spiritual manifestations, establish the mood by creating a sacred working space, and channel your magic.

CLEAR INTENTIONS

On the surface, manifestation is pretty simple – think about what you want to manifest, focus on it, and watch it come into your life – but when you break down each of these steps carefully, you will begin to understand why manifestation is such a challenge for most people. One of the main obstacles of manifestation is clarity. Having a clear vision about what you're calling in to your life is key for effective magic and potion making. Knowing what you want to manifest may seem like a no-brainer, but it can be quite complicated when you peel back the layers and look at the deeper motivations behind your surface-level goals.

Janet Bray Attwood and Chris Attwood repeat an amazing principle in their book *The Passion Test*, which speaks to the heart of clarity in manifestation. They say, "When you are clear, what you want will show up in your life, and only to the extent you are clear." Spirit is always waiting to give you exactly what you ask for, but if your desires are muddy and confusing then what you receive will also be such.

It's important to have total clarity before beginning any spirit formulation if your intention is to craft an effective, pleasing product. In Chapter 5, I outline a ritual to focus your mind, dig deeper into your goals, and find the clarity needed to create moon potions that are functional, intentional, and successful.

INVOKING THE SENSES

Ideally, the formulations you create will be your ritual partners for years to come. A good product should be effective and pleasing to the senses: an herbaceous perfume can garner compliments when you wear it and a naturally made full moon shampoo can have an amazing lather. Gone are the days when spiritual medicine had to mean something that smells funky or tastes awful. On the following pages, you are going to learn how to use the five material senses as well as one sacred one to create formulations that you'll want to use again and again.

Smell: Creating Fragrances

Fragrances are probably my favorite part of the crafting process and, in fact, I can pretty much trace this entire journey back to my love of aromatherapy and perfume. I believe a product should smell good no matter its function, and you can consistently create beautiful scents with a little bit of awareness and practice.

Knowing what kinds of scents you like is half the battle. Do you enjoy florals or woods, fresh or moody, or a combination of things? Commercial fragrances have a mix of different scent profiles, delivering a complex and intriguing scent that will change over time, but don't feel as though you have to mix dozens of scents together to find something special and unique. Two or three oil perfumes can be just as pleasing to the nose, and many of my bestsellers of all time are simple blends. I recommend purchasing perfume strips on Amazon, which make it easy to smell how two or more fragrances will interact with each other before blending them together.

There are plenty of ways to create fragrances, and I have tried many of them over the years. I find that my favorites are always ones that I intuitively created, simply looking at my list of choices and picking up the ones I feel most called to. The most important takeaway is to practice and have fun. You don't have to share these blends with anyone, so don't feel pressured to create anything specific. Even if you plan to sell your potions at some point you should enjoy what you create, and the crafting process is your opportunity to connect with your ingredients to make something that is uniquely your own. Below are my steps for creating fragrance blends using perfume strips.

Step 1: Make a list of essential oils that fit your product's intention and a few words about why you chose each one, then make a separate list for fragrance oils if you are using them. You'll want to start your fragrance with essential oils so you can add in your desired energy. Fragrances don't carry energetic properties and should be an afterthought to harmonize the blend.

Step 2: Write down the name of each oil on the perfume strips, one name for each strip.

Step 3: Dip the corresponding strip (the side without the name) into the bottle of essential or fragrance oil and lay them on a surface that won't interact with the chemicals in the fragrance. I use a steel table for this. Be sure to space them so that excess drips don't run into each other and cross contaminate the smell.

Step 4: Pick up two or more strips at a time, holding the bottom parts (the side with the name) together and forming a fan so there is about 1 in | 2.5 cm between each scented strip at the top.

Step 5: Wave them back and forth about 4 in | 10 cm in front of your nose and inhale. Place each strip back on its respective space on the table and write down your findings. Focus on your initial reaction to the fragrance, and whether that shifted slightly as you waved the strips back and forth. Was there one or more of the strips that seemed to disrupt an otherwise pleasing fragrance?

Step 6: Repeat steps 4 and 5 until you find a combination you enjoy.

Sight: Establishing a Mood

Merriam Webster defines "mood" as a conscious state of mind; a feeling, as well as a distinctive atmosphere. In a nutshell, the way your potions-crafting space looks has a profound impact on the way you feel and, as a result, the energy you infuse into your potions. The mood of your space can provoke romance or playfulness, coziness and warmth, and airiness and a feeling of wide open, clear energy.

Your sacred potions-making space is your safe haven where you can escape from the world and let your truest, deepest self emerge. Therefore, this space should reflect who you are at your core: A place that feels just as comfortable and familiar as the inner workings of your mind, body, and soul. You can create this level of comfort by focusing on the vibe around you as you work your moon potions. How do you want your potion to make you feel? How can you bring elements of that feeling into the room you'll be working in? As a guided person who always lives by what I'm feeling in my soul at any given moment, I love the idea of following the natural rhythms of the moon and bringing the energy of each moon cycle into my working space.

The basics don't change much: The furniture and the color of the walls stays the same. For the most part, photos and décor pieces I absolutely love are always adorning my space, but that doesn't mean I don't enjoy a refresh from season to season, month to month, or even moon phase to moon phase when that is practical. It doesn't need to be dramatic or overwhelming. Focus on the little things that are easy to change such as lighting different candles for different phases, setting up an aromatherapy diffuser with one of the essential oils that corresponds to the moon phase you're working with, or playing different kinds of music to promote your desired feeling.

For moon-potion making, I love my space to feel moody yet magical and just a little dark. There are times when I like to formulate under a full moon, but for the most part I'm crafting during the day and I'm sure the same will be true for you. That doesn't mean I can't welcome a little night-time energy into the space. Sometimes I'll draw the curtains and set candles all around me or I'll choose to work right at sunset. Now it's your turn: how do you want to feel?

Sound: Setting Your Apothecary Mood

Music, just like everything else, has a vibration, and sound can change your mood and therefore the vibe of your entire crafting process. When creating a potion for relaxation, consider playing music that makes you feel relaxed. The same goes for a potion that is meant to increase your energy or motivation: consider putting on a motivational speech audio or something that has an upbeat tune. A quick internet search will provide a plethora of background music to choose from.

See Bonus Material, page 265, to access links to some of my favorite videos and Spotify playlists.

Touch: Working with Textures

Textures will be most apparent in formulations such as lotions and creams, scrubs, and thicker liquids such as gels or oils, but even sprays and bath salts have a texture and shouldn't be overlooked. Everything you add to your potion can change the feeling of the end result. Some oils such as castor oil or olive oil are much thicker than others such as grapeseed or hazelnut. There are coarse salts and sugars but also fine ones and everything in between, and even essential oils can disrupt or alter the stability of a potion in some cases. Don't be alarmed: trial and error is part of the fun, but I do have some recommendations to help you avoid costly mistakes or wasting precious ingredients:

- Make smaller test batches first if you are unfamiliar with how an ingredient will affect your potion.

- Consider avoiding an ingredient that is irritating to your skin in its raw form. There is a good chance it will also be irritating to you, even if properly diluted or mixed into something else.

- Consider the type of product you'd like to make and what texture characteristics you're expecting to experience before adding anything to your blend. Feel the ingredient in its raw form where it is safe to do so. Does it match the texture of your desired final potion? For example, adding a powdered herb to a lotion might create a gritty texture that doesn't match a desired creamy feeling.

- Add ingredients in small amounts, mixing thoroughly between additions. You can always add more but you can't take it away.

- Use a whisk or fork for better incorporation.

- Can your ingredient be infused or diluted into something else before adding it to the final potion? For example, essential oils can break down shampoos, causing them to become thin and watery. Likewise, adding herbs directly to a water-based formula such as a shampoo can cause your potions to go moldy. Try infusing a herb or diluting an essential oil blend into an oil before adding it.

- Consult the recipes in this book as a reference on how much of each ingredient to add.

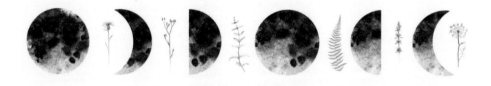

Here are some important things to keep in mind in addition to the tips above. Lotions and creams are oil and water emulsions that are easy to destabilize, especially if you are making the emulsions yourself. Store-bought lotions and creams can withstand a little more, but even these have a breaking point. Waters, oils and essential oils can all be mixed into a lotion or cream in liberal amounts, mixing well between each addition. However, too much of any of these can break down the lotion's chemical structure and cause the oil and water to separate.

Never add plant material directly to a lotion, as the water content within it can cause the plant material to go moldy. Infuse dry herbs into an oil first, then add liberal amounts as mentioned above.

Each liquid has its own weight and feel and can affect the way a spray feels on your skin. You might find certain alcohols or teas have a drying effect, while others may have more of a moisturizing feel.

Taste: Brew Up Something Magical

Even your drinks can be an opportunity to infuse an extra layer of moon magic into your potion-making processes. You might consider drinking chamomile for the new moon, cinnamon or ginger tea if you are making potions for the waxing moon, rose tea for the full moon, or peppermint for the lunar eclipse. Check out the beginning of each chapter in Part II to find a list of herbs for each moon phase, or make up a batch of the blend below for all of your magical moon making.

A SWEET MAGICAL MAKER'S TEA BLEND

- 1 tbs dried rose hips
- 1 tbs freeze-dried strawberries
- 1 tsp dried calendula flowers
- 1–2 orange slices
- 20 oz | 590 ml cold filtered water

Add the rose hips, strawberries, calendula and orange slices to a teapot with a strainer. You can also add the dried material to a large fillable teabag and place it along with the orange slices inside a teapot. Bring the water to a soft boil, then remove from heat and allow it to set for 1 minute. Pour the water into the teapot over the herb mixture and steep for 10 minutes. Sweeten with honey if desired and enjoy!

Spirit: You Are Your Own Sacred Tool

The most important sense your moon magic can have is you. Don't worry about getting things correct, because whether you know it or not your higher self is gently pushing you in the right direction, bringing the right ingredients to your awareness, and calling in whatever you need to be successful in your plans. Trust your intuition and know that experimenting is part of the process. I have made some of my most popular potions by accident and discovered innovative methods by messing up something else. Let your magic lead you, and stay open minded to discovering what you're capable of when you get out of your own way.

PART II

MOON RECIPES

The recipes in this book are my tried and true, all-time favorite moon recipes I have ever created. They are a combination of personal recipes I use at home and blends I have created for my spiritual apothecary over the years and they're pretty great, but I encourage you to use them as base recipes, switching out ingredients to fit your needs.

In each moon chapter you will find a short list of moon "correspondences" or ingredients, the vibration of which aligns with each respective moon phase. Use this as your starting list, replacing them with things from the recipes you'll find here. I encourage you to follow your intuition, selecting the ingredient you're most called to, then you can confirm your intuitive pings with the correspondence tables in Appendix I.

CHAPTER 5

NEW
MOON

The new moon shifts the energy from waning to waxing. It represents fresh beginnings, rebirth, and the dark void of potential. The moon isn't visible in the sky during this phase, making it the darkest nights of the moon cycle when all possibilities are waiting to be claimed. The lack of moonlight represents a clean slate, allowing you to fill that space with your wildest dreams. It's like the moon's version of a genie in a bottle, waiting to hear your wish, which is why the new moon phase is associated with dreaming up your wildest dreams and setting intentions with hopes of manifesting them into your life. In this chapter, you will find recipes and rituals to help you open your higher chakras for increased vision and guidance from your higher self, as well as recipes and rituals to take these visions and set your intentions. With a little bit of moon magic, you could be well on your way to calling in your deepest desires and becoming your future self.

VISION

Before you can set your intentions, you need an understanding of what your desires are. Magic always needs room for spontaneity and flow, but the universe likes it when you offer a specific starting point to build from. Spending time with your higher self is the best way to determine who you're becoming, allowing you to be really clear about what your manifestations should focus on. Your higher self has access to the spiritual realms and, therefore, spiritual intelligence, in a way that your conscious mind may never have. Connecting with your soul, specifically asking "Who am I becoming?", opens the door to possibilities you may not have considered, even if you feel as though you have a strong sense of what you want.

INTENTIONS

Once you have the vision, setting intentions becomes a lot easier and more specific. It may be tempting to try to manifest an entire life's work of desires in one moon phase, but focusing on one or two intentions at a time is most ideal. In theory, you'd set an intention during the new moon and it will manifest by the full moon; however, it's important to be realistic about the amount of time your intention needs to manifest. Some intentions will require several moon cycles and maybe even several years for the grandest goals, especially if you have found manifestation challenging in the past, but that doesn't mean you should avoid setting bigger intentions – as long as you are patient.

Don't overlook smaller intentions, as even small wins can help build the confidence and belief needed to manifest something huge like a new car or $1 million. Starting with something minuscule like manifesting an extra $100 expands your understanding of what is possible, and next time you can try something bigger like $500. Regardless of what you attempt to call in, remember that manifestation is a skill that anyone can learn but it may take time to do so. Don't give up if things don't start happening right away or you feel as though you're doing anything wrong. Your energy will call in the things you desire when the time is right. When you are feeling out of alignment with your goals, give the visualization technique over the page a try.

GETTING IN ALIGNMENT VISUALIZATION

Sit down in a quiet place and close your eyes. Take a few deep breaths to center yourself, then allow your breath to return to normal once you feel calm. Keeping your eyes closed, imagine a wavy horizontal stream of light emanating from your third eye. This is your vibration sending a call out to your desires.

Imagine another similar stream of light just above your head. Watch as the second stream above your head moves slowly towards the stream at your third eye. They may appear to move at different speeds at first, but as they grow closer they slowly begin to move in the same speed and shape, getting closer until they combine to form one energetic wave just in front of your third eye. Feel the vibration of your energy and the energy of your desires, matching their frequency and coming into alignment with each other. Stay there for several moments.

When you're ready, thank your desires for coming into alignment with your vibration and open your eyes.

Moon-Maker Tip: See Bonus Material, page 265, to access the audio recording of this visualization.

NEW MOON CORRESPONDENCES

Below is a list of ingredients and symbols that align with the energy of the new moon you can use as a starting point for creating your own lunar apothecary potions. Each ingredient has its own properties, bringing something unique to your magical potions. Be sure to check out the correspondence tables in Appendix I to discover the individual characteristics of each ingredient.

ESSENTIAL OILS	PLANTS	CRYSTALS
Bergamot	Balsam fir	Black moonstone
Chamomile	Bamboo	Black obsidian
Cinnamon	Chamomile	Citrine
Lemon	Cinnamon	Clear quartz
Myrrh	Clove	Himalayan salt
Neroli	Frankincense	Labradorite
Oakmoss	Honeysuckle	Smoky quartz
Opopanax	Tonka bean	
Orange		
Patchouli		
Sandalwood		

FUTURE-SELF VISUALIZATION RITUAL

I find one of the biggest obstacles to achieving goals is a lack of clarity and specificity. You may have a goal to be a millionaire but not have an idea of how you're going to achieve this. Sure, you can leave it up to chance, but the universe can respond with more ease when your goals are specific and clear.

This visualization ritual will introduce you to who you're becoming. Use this guidance to create a list of goals that support your future self. Be sure to gather as much information as you can while in mediation, asking questions about what do you do for a living, what kind of people have helped you accomplish these goals, and what obstacles you faced. The more information you have, the easier it will be to identify your next steps.

- 2 incense sticks

- clear quartz point or wand

- Third Eye–Activating Face Serum (page 67)

- clear quartz or amethyst face roller

- Crown Chakra Anointing Hair Oil (page 65)

- pen and paper

- a quiet place to meditate for 30 minutes

Step 1: Light the incense sticks using a heatproof incense holder and place it near your meditation space.

Step 2: Lay out the tools and potions you will be using during this ritual in front of your meditation space so they are easily accessible.

Step 3: Using a clear quartz crystal or wand, draw a big circle around you and your ritual tools to safely contain and raise your energy.

Step 4: Massage a few drops of the Third Eye Activating Face Serum onto your face, working in clockwise, circular motions, then use a quartz or amethyst roller to massage for a few minutes more, focusing on your brow bone and third eye, located just between your brows.

Step 5: Massage a small amount of Crown Chakra Anointing Hair Oil into the palms of your hands and fingertips. Take a moment to inhale the oil three times then gently massage the scalp, focusing on the very top of your head and applying more as needed.

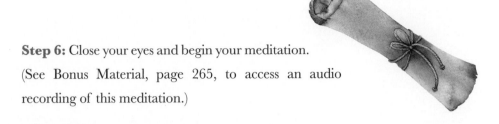

Step 6: Close your eyes and begin your meditation. (See Bonus Material, page 265, to access an audio recording of this meditation.)

Step 7: Write down as much as you can recall from the meditation and use this information to set intentions for the Planting Seeds Intention-Setting Ritual on page 63.

PLANTING SEEDS INTENTION–SETTING RITUAL

This ritual combines all of the things needed for successful manifestation. You have guidance from your future self for spirit planting, which is grounding and connecting your physical body to the earth, and of course the intentions themselves, bringing in the mind and heart with your desired outcome.

- DIY Seeded Intention-Setting Paper (see page 70)
- pen
- garden soil
- garden pot with drainage holes
- water

Be sure to do the Future-Self Visualization Ritual on page 61 before beginning this ritual.

Gather up the materials and set them in a quiet working space where it is comfortable to sit and write. Review the guidance from the Future-Self Visualization Ritual, then begin writing out two or three intentions in as much detail as possible on the DIY Seeded Intention-Setting Paper. Continue writing for at least 5 minutes – past where you think you are ready to stop, because you'll find there is often a little more to say.

Add enough garden soil to fill about three-quarters of the desired pot, then fold up the paper into a small pouch and place it on top of the soil. Add another 1–2 in | 2.5–5 cm of garden soil and water well.

Add a stick or label to the pot inscribed with the date it was planted and your intentions. Consult the seed package to find the best spot to grow your plant. Continue to nurture your plant and watch your intentions grow.

Moon-Maker Tip: Water your growing plant with Moon Water (see page 27) once a month on or just after a full moon.

Crown Chakra Anointing Hair Oil to Unlock the Upper Chakras

One of the very first connections I made between beauty products and spirituality was the undeniable connection between crown chakra ingredients and ingredients that are amazing for hair care. Many plants and herbs that stimulate and open the crown chakra, coincidentally (except I don't believe in coincidences), are nourishing, stimulating, or encourage hair growth. It seemed like a natural fit, and I've been making variations of crown chakra shampoo, conditioner, and this hair oil for many years.

This oil will gently nudge open your upper chakras, specifically your crown chakra, to allow your higher self to communicate with you more clearly for guidance and direction. Use this oil for the Future-Self Visualization Ritual on page 61.

- 1 tbs dried lavender flowers
- 1 tbs dried blue lotus (or rose petals if not available)
- 1 tsp gotu kola powder
- 1 cup olive oil
- 20 drops of cedarwood
- 20 drops of lavender
- 20 drops of rosewood
- amethyst or quartz gemstone

Put the herbs and olive oil in a small crockpot, cover and turn on the lowest setting. Alternatively, put the herbs and olive oil in a heatproof glass jar or measuring cup and put it into a saucepan with about 3 in | 7.5 cm of water and turn on low. Allow the mixture to gently warm for 1 hour then turn off the heat. Once cooled, strain the oil and compost the herb material. Pour the oil into a dark-colored 8 oz | 240 ml bottle, then add the essential oils and crystal. Store in a dark place and shake well before use.

To use, massage a small amount in the palms of your hands and fingertips and gently massage into your scalp. Rub the remaining oil from your palms down the length of your hair, focusing most of the oil on the ends. Apply more as needed and shampoo out if desired.

THIRD EYE–ACTIVATING FACE SERUM

Like the crown chakra and hair there is a fair amount of connection between third eye ingredients and ingredients that are good for both the face and sinuses. The essential oils used in this recipe are balancing for the skin and also happen to open your third eye chakra for increased intuition, vision, and spiritual understanding. Sometimes before meditation I like to rub a few drops on my face then massage with an amethyst face roller, focusing on the third eye area just between my brow bones. Use this oil for the Future-Self Visualization Ritual on page 61.

- 8 drops of sandalwood essential oil

- 7 drops of carrot seed essential oil

- 5 drops of rose essential oil

- 2 drops of clary sage essential oil

- 1 very small amethyst gemstone, optional

- 2 tbs jojoba oil

- 2 tbs walnut oil

- 1 tsp almond oil

- 1 tsp vitamin E oil

Add the essential oils to a 2 oz | 60 ml, dark-colored bottle that has a hole big enough to slide the gemstone through. After adding the gem, top off with the base oils and shake to combine. Allow the oils to synergize for at least one day and shake well before use.

A little of this oil goes a long way. Massage a few drops on your face in a clockwise, circular motion. Be sure to spend a little extra time massaging the oil into your third eye area.

FRAGRANCED INCENSE STICKS

I absolutely love incense sticks but sometimes I find readily available fragrances to be extremely overpowering, plus they're often made with toxic fragrance oils that do not have any spiritual properties. Making fragranced incense sticks is super easy: the ingredients are readily available online, and you can customize the essential oil blend to fit your intentions.

- 1 tbs blend of new moon essential oil or oils of your choice
- 2 tbs dipropylene glycol (DPG)
- 15 unscented incense sticks

Combine the essential oil blend with the DPG, then pour into a shallow dish or bowl that is big enough to accommodate the length of the entire incense sticks. Dip each stick in the mixture and turn several times to make sure each side is covered.

Remove the sticks from the fragrance mixture and lay each one flat on a drying rack for 24 hours. To use, light the tip and allow it to burn for 30 seconds, then blow it out and place it in an incense-stick holder to continue burning.

> *Moon-Maker Tip*: Try using unscented
> charcoal incense cones in place of the sticks,
> following the same instructions above.

You can replace essential oils with clean fragrance oils, but remember that although they do not have spiritual properties they do make for a wonderful scented experience.

DIY SEEDED INTENTION–SETTING PAPER

Making paper is fun and easier than you might think, and "planting" my intentions is one of my favorite things to do because it requires love and nurturing to make sure the plant grows. You're reaffirming your intentions every time you tend to your plant, plus you can choose seeds to grow plants that correspond with your intentions.

- recyclable eco-friendly paper
- warm water
- seeds
- towel or flannel fabric

Tear or shred the paper into small pieces (I used a paper shredder), then fill a blender about halfway. Pour enough warm water to reach the max line of the blender, then put the top on and blend on low for 10 to 20 seconds. Increase the speed and blend for another 30 seconds to 1 minute. All of the paper should be pulp at this point, but go ahead and blend again for 30 seconds at a time as needed until no more paper flakes can be seen.

Pour in the seeds and mix well with a spoon or spatula. Do not use the blender for this as the seeds will be cut up and they won't grow. Pour the mixture through a thin mesh strainer, and press the pulp using a spoon to strain out as much liquid as possible.

Lay out the towel as flat as possible and spoon some of the mixture on top. Use a spoon or spatula to spread the mixture into the shape and size desired, making the layer as thin as possible: the thicker the layer, the thicker the paper. Use a dry sponge to flatten the paper and absorb excess moisture. Continue this process of adding and spreading the pulp on the fabric until all of the pulp is used up.

Allow the sheets to dry on one side then turn the sheets over on another dry piece of fabric to dry on the other side. Allow both sides to dry out completely, then use them as you would regular paper or in the Planting Seeds Intention-Setting Ritual below.

The sheets of paper can be printed on but try to use eco-friendly ink where possible, especially if you are using seeds for edible plants. You don't want any toxic compounds growing in your plants that are intended for food. The same goes for the type of paper used to make the sheets.

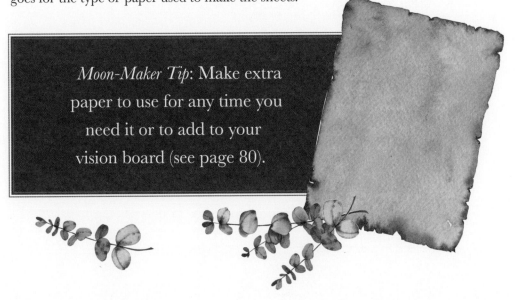

Moon-Maker Tip: Make extra paper to use for any time you need it or to add to your vision board (see page 80).

GENERAL NEW MOON BATH

This bath is a great base for your next new moon bathing ritual and can be customized as you see fit. Just make sure to blend this up about a week before the new moon so that it has time to synergize and deepen its magic. This recipe makes enough for about four to eight baths depending on how much you use, so you'll have it for a while.

- 2 cups alcohol (see the notes on the opposite page)
- 1 tsp vanilla extract
- 5 drops of petitgrain essential oil
- 4 drops of patchouli chamomile essential oil
- 1 drops of vetiver essential oil
- 1 tbs carrier oil (see notes below)
- clear quartz crystals
- black or navy candles, optional to set the mood for your working table or space or during your bath

Pour all of the ingredients into a dark-colored bottle large enough to hold the mixture, along with one or two pieces of clear quartz. Screw on a tight-fitting lid and gently shake to combine. Allow this mixture to synergize in a dark cabinet for about seven days, shaking occasionally.

> *Moon-Maker Tip*: Alcohol is great for exfoliating and softening skin, although it tends to be overlooked because of the cost. You don't need anything expensive, as a cheap bottle will do nicely.

Notes: Any type of drinking alcohol will work, but my personal favorite is brandy because it adds its own extra layer of fragrance. I also find rum to be a nice addition, but whiskey, vodka, gin, tequila, and even wine or cordials will do. Just be mindful of the wine, because it can stain the tub. Vinegar can be used if you'd prefer not to use alcohol. White vinegar is my personal favorite, or you can use champagne vinegar if you'd like a little extra pampering.

Vegetable oils have metaphysical properties just as crystals and plants do. I often change the carrier oil I use for the recipe once I run out and need to make a new batch. Olive oil is great for wealth, while sunflower is a powerful oil for promoting positivity and happiness. Grapeseed oil is similar to clear quartz in the sense that it can be programmed to hold any intention, making it a great choice for a variety of intentions.

CHAPTER 6

WAXING CRESCENT MOON

PLANNING

The waxing crescent moon represents small steps forward. If you turn your gaze to the night sky during this phase you will see a small sliver of the moon, with just enough light to be visible. The growth may be minimal, yet you know that over time this small crescent will grow to a full display of lunar energy. Taking a step forward, no matter how small, is *you* putting that same faith into your desires and the universe's ability to deliver them.

The next natural step after setting an intention is creating a plan to bring that goal into physical form. The universe will do most of the work for you, but remember that you also have a critical part to play in your desired outcome – whether that is googling career options, making a wish list of supplies to buy to fulfill a hobby, practicing taking selfies until you have a cache of options for a dating site, or declaring a desire to a friend just to say it out loud. Spending money isn't always the way to take a step forward, and often it's the small cost-free things that are the hardest to invest in.

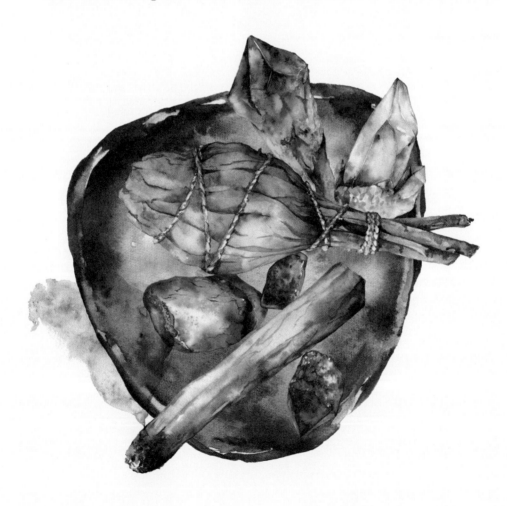

WAXING CRESCENT MOON CORRESPONDENCES

Below is a list of ingredients and symbols that align with the energy of the waxing crescent moon you can use as a starting point for creating your own lunar apothecary potions. Each ingredient has its own properties, bringing something unique to your magical potions. Be sure to check out the correspondence tables in Appendix I to discover the individual characteristics of each ingredient.

ESSENTIAL OILS	PLANTS	CRYSTALS
Angelica	Elder berries and flowers	Carnelian
Anise	Five finger grass	Green aventurine
Benzoin	Milk thistle	Moss agate
Clary sage	Oak	
Geranium	Peach	
Juniper	Sage	
Lemon balm	Sunflower	
Mugwort		
Oakmoss		
Palmarosa		
Peppermint		
Tea tree		
Thyme		

Ginger, Lime, and Red Blossom Tea

I struggle with a lot of anxiety when I'm ready to plan out a goal, and I'm sure you've dealt with your fair share of doubt, fear, and frustration too. This tea blend has a calming effect, and the ingredients used all correspond to the energies of success, confidence, and spiritual strength. I like to brew up a cup when I'm working on vision boards.

- 1 cup cold water
- 1 in | 2.5 cm piece ginger, sliced
- 1 tsp dried red clover blossoms
- 1–2 lime slices

Bring the water to a boil, then add the ginger and reduce to a simmer. Cook for 10 minutes. Put the red clover blossoms in a teabag or strainer and place inside a mug along with the lime. Pour the boiling ginger water over the teabag and lime and allow to steep for a further 10 minutes. Enjoy!

Moon-Maker Tip: You can enjoy this blend as a syrup base for soda. Make a simple syrup by mixing equal parts water and granulated sugar in a small saucepan. Add the herbs and bring to a soft boil until the sugar has completely melted. Remove from heat and allow it to cool. Add 1–2 oz | 30–60 ml of syrup to a glass and top with sparkling water in a flavor of your choice. I like La Croix in lime or passionfruit flavors.

HERBS TO BURN WHILE PLANNING

Below is a selection of herbs and resins to burn while planning or vision boarding. Each of the items on this list carries the energy of success or helps to reduce the anxiety that can sometimes happen when tackling a big goal:

- bay leaf
- benzoin
- chamomile
- cinnamon
- ginger
- honeysuckle
- lemon balm
- mustard seed
- pine.

To use, light a charcoal incense disk until it begins to crackle and turn orange then place it on a flameproof dish in a well ventilated room. Sprinkle a pinch or two of incense onto the disk. It will begin to smoke as it burns. Allow the incense to continue to burn, adding another pinch if desired to reinvigorate the smoke.

> *Moon-Maker Tip*: Select the herb based solely on your intuition without making any effort to look up the meaning or spiritual properties. Go on to plan your goals, then once you are done look up the meaning of these herbs and see if it corresponds with your intention.

CREATING THE PERFECT VISION BOARD

A couple of years ago, I went on a weekend trip with a friend to make vision boards for the new year. To my surprise, she was making a vision board for the first time despite having been in the spiritual community for as long as I've known her: nearly a decade. She said she didn't really know what a vision board was or how to do one, so of course I started wondering how many people have similar experiences. I started asking people whether they made vision boards and, if so, whether they felt as though they worked. More importantly, I asked if they worked for the individual. What I found is that most people have made a vision board of some kind, but almost all of them felt as though they didn't make a difference when it came to manifesting.

I was shocked, because my vision boards always manifest in some way or another – maybe not the whole board, but definitely most. I will admit that many of my earlier boards didn't work, and I would say the biggest reason for those failed boards was not having a list of what I wanted on them. I would start looking for images without a clear understanding of what I was looking for, so I ended up with a hodgepodge of a lot of things I didn't really care about. The second biggest reason was not having a variety of goals: I only added really big goals that required a significant quantum leap to achieve. It's a good idea to have one or two big goals, as you'll discover later on in this chapter, but it's also really important to have smaller, easier goals because doing so will build your confidence. Think of it as a manifestation savings account: you may not be able to deposit a huge amount right away but you can save up over time. The same goes for manifesting: you may not be able to achieve those big dreams straight out the gate, but you can work towards building your manifestation capabilities.

Ultimately, better vision boards can be achieved with awareness and some planning. I've been making vision boards for a very long time now and I have picked up some really helpful tips along the way, in addition to what I have mentioned above, which are what I want to share with you here.

WHAT IS A VISION BOARD?

Think of a vision board as a scrapbook of sorts for your future self: it is a visual representation of the things you'd like to have in your life. The point of a vision board is to be a regular reminder of your intentions, kind of like saying a daily affirmation but in physical form where you can actually see a representation of what you want.

For one, it gives you a moment of "Oh, yeah, I should be working towards this goal." Additionally, it gives your subconscious mind a visual point of reference. Every time you look at it, your mind takes a snapshot and goes "Got it, this is what you want," and your subconscious mind starts to influence you and your decisions in a way that helps you to attain your goals.

SUPPLIES FOR A VISION BOARD

Pictures: The most important thing is the pictures. You can cut out photos from magazines or print them online. My favorite place to source images is Pinterest, but you can also google them or take screenshots from your favorite website and social pages. You can also try cutting out or printing words and quotes. I like to make a list of keywords that represent various things on my board and then type them out in Canva with a pretty font, leaving space between each line. I then download, print and cut the words out and use them as filler space on my board.

Physical things: At one point, I was putting physical tarot cards on my vision board such as the 10 of Pentacles when I wanted to make more money. I decided to redo my wardrobe a few years back, so I added tags from clothes I've gotten as well as strips of the kinds of fabrics I wanted to wear. The sky's the limit, as long as it represents your goals and isn't too heavy to stay attached. Here are some suggestions to get you started:

- crystals and shells
- dried flowers and plants
- fabric swatches for furniture or clothes
- interior design samples: this is great for manifesting home renovations, but make sure they aren't too heavy or use something that is strong enough to support heavier materials
- jewelry
- tickets for travel or concerts
- pamphlets and brochures.

Boards: I like to make my boards on canvas, which I get packs of from my local craft store. Pretty much any craft store will have canvas as well as foam or poster board, which are both great options, but you can also get creative. I've made vision boards from cork boards with photos tacked on, and one year I got really ambitious and put each picture in a photo frame and made a gallery wall in my bedroom. I wanted the images to feel like memories or as though I already had these things. It was a lot of work, but it also worked well. Pretty much any sturdy board will do, even cardboard from the side of a box.

Adhesive: Which adhesive you use is really going to depend on what you're putting on your board. I don't like using regular glue, even on regular pieces of paper. I find they peel after a while and I prefer to use a hot glue gun, especially when I'm adding things such as crystals or something stronger than regular paper, but any adhesive that works for you is fine.

Hanging materials: Finally, you'll want a way to hang your board if you're planning on putting it up on the wall. I use heavy-duty hooks that I get from a hardware store that go into the wall at an angle so you can use them on drywall. They are sometimes called drywall hooks, I believe, but if you go to a hardware store and tell them you want to hang something heavy on drywall they will know what you're talking about. I use hooks because I hang canvas, but if you're using a foam board you can use something like command strips or even nail them directly into the wall. Just make sure that you pick a spot where you'll see your vision board daily. Of course, you don't have to hang your board at all. You can prop it up against a wall with a selection of other art prints or, if it's smaller, you can keep it on a desk or table.

THIS IS YOUR VISION

Again, there is no right or wrong way to make a vision board. This is *your* vision, and what you choose to put on it is entirely up to you. That's why I think it's a good idea to vision board by yourself if you're someone who's easily influenced, or if you're confused and maybe don't have a clear understanding of what your vision is. Otherwise, someone else might influence you or talk you into putting up something you don't actually want, in which case you probably won't manifest it because it isn't something you truly feel your spirit is called to. That can lead to you feeling insecure about the process, which could hurt your manifestation power in the long run.

You can make your vision boarding a whole experience. Create a vibe or create a mood, and do this when you feel good and relaxed and, above all, inspired. This whole process should be fun and should light a bit of a fire under your butt and get you motivated. The most important thing is being honest about what you want – but more on this later in this chapter.

THE ELEPHANT IN THE ROOM: LIFE HAPPENS!

There are many vision boards from the pandemic that didn't manifest *at all*, because no one was prepared for a world pandemic and, of course, no one knew how to create a mood board that took a world pandemic into consideration. For example, I wanted to travel and open a coffee shop in 2020, and by late February I had three trips booked. Technically, I did manifest my trips but, ultimately, they were all canceled in light of the Covid situation. There's nothing you or I can do about situations such as that, but there is a greater plan that transcends any one person and, indeed, transcends entire communities. In this case, there was a greater plan for the whole world.

Before you make a vision board, just know that you didn't fail at manifesting when things are beyond your control. Your intentions transcend time and space and won't always fit neatly into a year or moon phase. In the case of Covid, I know that in the end not going on trips was for my highest good, because it meant not getting sick or potentially exposing my family or employees to Covid. And I'm okay with that. The same thing with the coffee shop: it just wouldn't be smart in my opinion to try to open a brand-new coffee shop when restaurants all over the country, and especially in LA, were closing permanently.

That doesn't mean I won't ever be able to manifest these things or that I should remove them from my vision board. It just means now is not the time and I should continue to hold the vision.

KNOW WHAT YOU WANT

This probably seems like a no-brainer to some, but knowing what you want isn't always so easy. You may think you know your desires until you sit down to pull pictures, and suddenly you hit a blank wall. Before making a vision board, be sure you are clear on your vision. Revisit Chapter 6 for tips on identifying your intentions.

Say you are vision boarding with your friend who is super clear about her vision for the next year, and part of that vision is getting a new Lexus. She makes a comment about how your car is kind of old and perhaps you should add a new car to your board too, but you love your car and up until that point you weren't even thinking about getting a new one. Yes, it may be older but it runs well, is in good shape, and is paid off. You're in no rush to change it. Buuuuuttt, then, you think about how your friend has a great body, always gets attention from people, has great hair, and now she's going to have a luxury car to match. Suddenly you're comparing yourself with her and you feel as though you don't measure up, so you print out a picture of a Lexus and add it to your vision board when you don't even want a new car – you just feel the pressure to do so.

I highly recommend doing this on your own first if you have a tendency to compare yourself with others. At the very least, be ultra clear about your vision before sharing it with someone else so you know what you want without a doubt.

Break Up Your List into Sections

When I make my list I arrange things by categories, as doing so helps me get a better understanding of which category needs the most work. Career might have 10 things, whereas fitness only has one or two. That means my career needs more space on my board because there are more things I feel I need there to be happy.

I find this practice to be super illuminating because sometimes I sit down to make a list and I think health or spirituality is going to be the most important thing, but then I break things up and realize that where I'm really seeking growth is in relationships or my finances. It's just another way to gain absolute clarity, and the more clarity you have the easier manifestation becomes.

Add Little Things

Vision boards are great for big things such as a new career, meeting a personal goal like having 10 k followers on YouTube, or losing weight, but don't discredit the little things. Achieving things feels good; even small victories can have a huge impact on your self-esteem and therefore your ability to have more confidence to manifest the bigger things.

Adding smaller intentions to the list like not hitting snooze on the alarm three days a week or taking the stairs instead of the elevator is a quick and easy way to build confidence and self-control, and to remind yourself that you alone have the power to change your life for the better. Also, it helps to look at your vision board and be able to say "Yes, I've achieved five things already," even if they are five little things.

Add Something Big

It's as important to add *big* things as it is to add little things. I add one seemingly unattainable thing every single year. In 2018 it was getting an oracle deck publishing deal. At the beginning of the year that seemed like the most far-fetched possibility ever, but I got it and now I have seven published oracles and at least three more contracts still to finish. In 2019 it was getting a new car. At the beginning of the year, I thought there was no way I'd be able to afford a car and continue to make the payments. I didn't have an abundance mindset, and I thought for sure I'd have to wait a few more years. Yet in November 2019, I got a brand-new car with, I kid you not, 9 miles on it. Fresh! Brand new!!

Adding that impossible thing to your vision board gives you a sense of "What if?", and every time you look at it your subconscious says: "Okay, let me see how we can make this happen." Just don't go crazy with the big things. It's important to have a healthy mix of small, medium, and large intentions and maybe one extra large.

I know a lot of teachers will tell you, you can manifest it all and truly I believe you can, but most people cannot go from manifesting zero to manifesting $ million. Just like you can't jog for 10 minutes today and expect to lose 20 pounds by the morning, manifestation is a spiritual muscle that needs to be strengthened before you pick up the heavy weights or you might hurt your process before really getting started.

BEYOND THE BOARD

Let's talk about vision boards that have nothing to do with boards at all. Vision boards are great, but you may spend a lot of time in your office and want to have your annual vision there, or perhaps you're someone who's always on your phone while on the go. Why not keep your visions there too?

A board is just the beginning: you can make all kinds of vision "boards." For example, I make a collage for my desktop background and one for my iPhone that is a smaller, more-focused version of my bigger board. You can even make cell phone cases through online print-on-demand places and add your own photos, which keeps your visions right in your face where you can see them all the time.

Also consider keeping a smaller version of your vision board in your planner. Take pages that you didn't use for your big board and glue them on the pages of the planner. The more places you see your vision the more chances your subconscious has to recognize the importance of these goals, and to start making shifts to draw them to you. Here are some additional suggestions:

- Print your vision board on the cover of a notebook using Canva.

- Break your vision boards into smaller parts and use the images to print a calendar. Each month, you'll see a different part of your vision hanging on the wall.

- Have your vision board printed onto a coffee mug or water bottle.

- Make a collage on Canva and use your vision board as TV artwork.

- Save your vision board images to a digital frame so they play throughout the day.

- Print out and laminate vision boards and use them as folder dividers.

- Get creative: there are plenty of other products on which you can print your vision board. Just be sure that you are using your vision-board creations for personal use. You cannot use someone else's images to sell without their express permission.

ESTHETIC MATTERS

Everyone has a personal vibe. You may not feel that way, but deep down you know what kind of esthetic you like. You may like country chic or bright pink and glitter, or modern and minimalist. Be honest and ask yourself whether you are going to enjoy looking at a vision board that is 50 shades of the rainbow if your preferred vibe is neutral. Probably not. Not only that, but the board wouldn't be an accurate representation of how you live your life or the goals you have.

Imagine walking through your super minimal space and seeing a cluttered color catastrophe on the wall. It's going to be out of place because it doesn't match your vibe. Say you want to buy a house but you print out a photo of a super-modern, sharp-lined home when you really want an A-line cabin–like cottage. Having a photo of a home that doesn't accurately represent what you want creates conflict within your spirit and ultimately the universe. You want your board to look as close to your real life as you possibly can.

Instead, look for images that match your current life or the life you wish to have. Choose colors, shapes, textures, and styles that accurately reflect your desired mood. You're probably only going to glance at this board for a few seconds in passing, so make them count. Clarity manifests; confusion does not.

SOURCE FROM REAL LIFE

Say you want to buy a house and there's one little house you pass by every day when going to work. Pull over one day and take a photo of it, print it out and put it on your board. You already love this house so seeing it on your vision board at home will bring you a little moment of joy, and it's in that moment that the universe is going to get the signal that this is what you want. You may even manifest that exact house – you never know.

If there are clothes you want to wear, go to the website and screenshot or save the images. If there's a company you want to work for, see if you can take a selfie in the lobby of the building, because doing so will give you a genuine feeling of having already manifested that goal. The point is to try to make your vision board as realistic for you as possible, and these little tweaks can make all the difference and help you to start seeing these visions as realistic and possible for you.

CHANNEL YOUR INNER GRAPHIC DESIGNER

Altering an image using Photoshop, Canva, PicMonkey, or other design programs is an easy way to up your visualization practice. When I wanted to get my book deals, I took pictures of books from my favorite authors and Photoshopped my name on the cover to make it look as though I was the author. When I wanted to make more money, I took a screenshot of my bank balance and Photoshopped a completely different figure. It looked exactly like my real bank app but with different numbers.

Yay! By now you should be set to make an amazing vision board and maybe even a few. Let's review what you've learned:

1. A vision board is like a snapshot of your future self. It's a way for you to get a visual sense of what your life could look like in just a few months.

2. A vision board is *your* vision, and there are all sorts of ways you can make vision boards your own. Try different materials such as canvas, cardboard, or foam board and even add unexpected items such as crystals, postcards, or even mementos.

3. Sometimes life happens. That doesn't mean you can't manifest something, but it may mean you can't do it right now. Don't give up hope. As long as you've been able to manifest at least one thing on your board, you are doing better than most people in the world who either don't know what manifestation is or simply can't do it.

4. Know what you want. Being clear is the best way to create the best possible board.

5. Make a list and break it up into sections to gain even more clarity before looking for photos.

6. Be sure to add big, medium, and small goals and don't forget to add one extra-large, almost impossible goal to give yourself a challenge.

7. Make more than one board if you need to and get creative about where you keep your vision boards. Remember that it doesn't have to be a board at all.

8. Esthetic matters. Go for colors and elements that match your life, which will make it easier to envision yourself achieving your goals.

9. Finally, a few minutes in Photoshop can really make a difference and uplevel your board's images.

CHAPTER 7

FIRST QUARTER MOON

The first quarter moon is your time to shine. You've dreamed the big dream and have your plan ready to go, and you've done your research, rehearsed your lines, and gone over every detail with a fine-toothed comb. Now it's time to put that planning into action. *Start making moves!* This phase also tends to bring up challenges that can create blocks. Action is a chance to have courage in the face of fear, a chance to break through your resistance and move forward. The potions and ritual found in this chapter will help you overcome doubts so you can take action with courage. Just remember that courage doesn't mean a lack of fear, but moving ahead despite your fears.

ACTION

Taking action can be empowering, liberating, and exciting but it can also be overwhelming and scary. Getting the ball rolling is one of the hardest steps in achieving a goal. It requires you to make a commitment to something and take a leap of faith, not knowing whether the action you are taking is correct. Forward movement also comes with a fair amount of change in most cases, because what is the point of action if not to change your current situation?

In the face of action you might find yourself thinking about all of the negative outcomes and how any choice you make can end in destruction. Every action comes with good and bad, but so does every inaction. There is a certain amount of risk with everything you do or don't do. Know that you have all you need to take the right risks when you follow your instincts and intuition.

FIRST QUARTER MOON CORRESPONDENCES

Below is a list of ingredients and symbols that align with the energy of the first quarter moon you can use as a starting point for creating your own lunar apothecary potions. Each ingredient has its own properties, bringing something unique to your magical potions. Be sure to check out correspondence tables in Appendix I to discover the individual characteristics of each ingredient.

ESSENTIAL OILS	PLANTS	CRYSTALS
Allspice	Allspice	Carnelian
Basil	Cedar leaf	Pyrite
Bergamot	Ginger	Tiger's eye
Cardamom	High John	
Cinnamon	Honeysuckle	
Clove	Motherwort	
Ginger	Yarrow	
Lemon	Vervain	
Lime		
Pepper		
Peppermint		
Petitgrain		
Pine		
Rosemary		
Sage		
Vetiver		

Finding Your Inner Light Ritual

Your inner light is something that must be nurtured and maintained, even if you're a really confident person. Intentionally tending to your light reminds you of your value and how much you have to share with the world. This simple ritual will encourage self-love and a healthy inner landscape. Work the ritual when you're ready to move your plans ahead but are experiencing self-doubt or apprehension, and then at least once a month moving forward to keep your confidence high.

- 3 tealights
- flower petals, optional
- rose quartz or other love-encouraging crystals, optional
- Boss Witch Perfume (see page 102)

Set aside 10 to 20 minutes for yourself when you can be alone and undisturbed. Place the candle trio in a single line on top of your altar or the surface you're using – the order doesn't matter – ensuring the surface you place them on is heatproof. If you're using the flowers and crystals, sprinkle them around the candles to lightly cover the altar space. The flowers and crystals will add a little extra layer of magic and care to this ritual but are not necessary.

Roll the perfume over the inside of your wrists, inhale the scent and take a few deep breaths to center yourself. Light the first candle and say:

This candle represents self-compassion. My mistakes do not represent who I am. I lovingly release my past and make room for a beautiful future.

Take a few more deep breaths and embrace the feeling of self-compassion. Light the second candle and say:

This candle represents my worth. I have so much value to offer the world. I trust in myself and nurture my sacred talents.

Take a few more deep breaths and embrace the feeling of worth. Light the third candle and say:

This candle represents self-love. I embrace who I am. The more I live authentically, the more my inner light grows. The more my inner light grows, the more aligned with my purpose I become.

Take a few deep breaths and embrace the feeling of love. Close your eyes and meditate upon these phrases, repeating them if you feel called to. Take a few more deep breaths when you're ready to return to the room and open your eyes. Allow the candles to burn down completely.

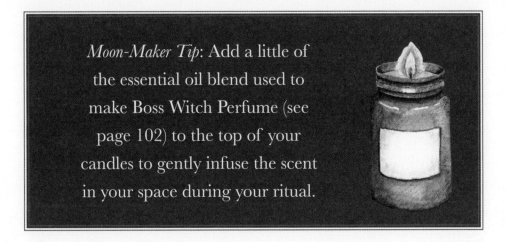

Moon-Maker Tip: Add a little of the essential oil blend used to make Boss Witch Perfume (see page 102) to the top of your candles to gently infuse the scent in your space during your ritual.

St. John's Energy Tincture

I always have a bottle of St. John's wort energy tincture on hand. I'll never forget the first time I heard evolutionary herbalist Sajah Popham mentioned how his teacher, famed herbalist Matthew Wood, said something along the lines of "It brings sunniness into the soul." There is evidence to support this herb's ability to ease mild depression. I like to add a few drops to water when I need a boost of confidence or vitality.

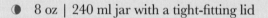

- 8 oz | 240 ml jar with a tight-fitting lid
- dried or fresh St. John's wort
- high-proof alcohol such as Everclear
- wax paper
- cheesecloth or coffee filters
- amber-colored dropper bottles

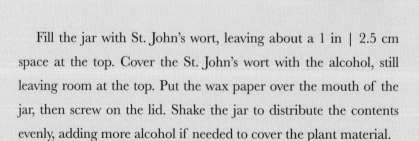

Fill the jar with St. John's wort, leaving about a 1 in | 2.5 cm space at the top. Cover the St. John's wort with the alcohol, still leaving room at the top. Put the wax paper over the mouth of the jar, then screw on the lid. Shake the jar to distribute the contents evenly, adding more alcohol if needed to cover the plant material.

Label the jar with the name and date and place it somewhere dark. Shake the jar every day for two to four weeks: the longer it sits, the more potent it will be. Strain the plant material through cheesecloth, pressing out as much of the liquid as possible. Compost the plant material. Pour the tincture into the dropper bottles and label.

To use, add 20 to 30 drops to a glass of cold water and drink as needed for an uplifted spirit and positive energy when you know you'll have a tough day, and for motivation to get you through the day.

Moon-Maker Tip: St. John's wort can be toxic when large amounts are ingested. Do not drink this tincture for more than one month at a time. A good rule of thumb is one month on, one month off. St. John's wort may impact the absorption of certain drugs, so be sure to check with a qualified doctor or medical professional before ingesting St. John's wort or any other herbal preparations.

BOSS WITCH PERFUME

There's something about this perfume that really makes me feel like I can tackle the day. I stopped offering this perfume years ago because of the cost and availability of vanilla, but I get asked to bring it back all the time and, truthfully, it is still one of my favorite fragrances. I love vanilla, and it pairs so perfectly with the lime. I added citrine to the bottles when I sold them but you can leave that out if desired or pack them to the rim. Follow your intuition.

- 15 drops of vanilla absolute essential oil
- 7 drops of patchouli essential oil
- 5 drops of lime essential oil
- 1 vitamin E capsule
- citrine chips, optional
- ⅓ oz | 10 ml jojoba oil

Drop the essential oils into a ⅓ oz | 10 ml perfume roller or small dropper bottle. Prick the vitamin E capsule with a needle and squeeze the contents into the bottle, then slip in the desired amount of citrine chips. Fill the bottle with the jojoba oil, push in the roller top and cap tightly. Gently shake to blend, then place the bottle on your altar to synergize for eight days. To use, roll onto your pulse points, behind your ears, décolletage, and bust. This blend can be used in an aromatherapy diffuser if desired.

Moon-Maker Tip: You can easily make this into a spray perfume by replacing the jojoba oil with 1 oz | 30 ml of high-proof alcohol such as Everclear.

CHAPTER 8

WAXING GIBBOUS MOON

The waxing gibbous moon is bittersweet. On the one hand it's a sign that you are very near to completion, but on the other this phase can bring about feelings of anxiousness, doubt, and analysis paralysis. You might experience this phase as an endless stream of mental chatter, second-guessing yourself and feeling the sudden need to make changes, or even an urge to quit something altogether. While all of these feelings are frustrating, they are likely a sign that you are just about to experience a breakthrough and/or a leveling up, and you should pause before making any significant changes.

This chapter was created for taking a break. Everything you find here will encourage patience and restore hope, but will mostly give your mind something to do other than trying to sabotage your progress.

PATIENCE

Many things can happen between having an idea and seeing that idea through. You may feel as though you need to rethink your strategy, idea, or even the direction of your life. Questions about whether you are enough or made the right choice can and often do come up, and it can be the case even if your goal is going smoothly. Remember that slow progress is still progress, and even the most successful people have doubts. Hold steady to your vision and don't give up hope.

WAXING GIBBOUS MOON CORRESPONDENCES

Below is a list of ingredients and symbols that align with the energy of the waxing gibbous moon you can use as a starting point for creating your own lunar apothecary potions. Each ingredient has its own properties, bringing something unique to your magical potions. Be sure to check out the correspondence tables in Appendix I to discover the individual characteristics of each ingredient.

ESSENTIAL OILS	PLANTS	CRYSTALS
Angelica root	Carnation	Angelite Citrine
Balsam fir	Cilantro	Blue lace agate
Basil	Coffee	Howlite
Cananga	Coriander	Rose quartz
Cedarwood	Gardenia	Sodalite
Chamomile	Heather	Unakite
Fennel	Lavender	
Hemlock spruce	Mustard seed	
Hyssop	Myrrh	
Jasmine	Olive leaf	
Lemongrass	Passionflower	
Palmarosa	Peppermint	
Rose	Rose	
	Sweetgrass	

Patience Floral Bath and Body Oil

I believe hope and beauty go hand in hand. Sometimes life can feel ugly, draining and overwhelming, yet a beautiful song, image, shared moment, or art can bring someone to tears and bring the light back to their soul. I created this body oil to be beautiful, claiming and, of course, crafted with herbs and oils that promote patience, hope and light.

- bouquet of fresh or dried carnations
- dried or fresh borage flowers
- 1 small aquamarine crystal, optional
- 1 small rose quartz crystal, optional
- 11 drops of hemlock spruce essential oil
- 5 drops of geranium essential oil
- 4 drops of lavender essential oil
- 1 drop of clove essential oil
- 1 drop of basil essential oil
- 1 drop of peppermint essential oil
- 1 vitamin E capsule
- 8 oz | 240 ml fractionated coconut oil

Rinse the fresh flowers and allow them to dry completely. You can skip this step if you are using dried-flower material.

Place the aquamarine and rose quartz crystals in an 8 oz | 240 ml bottle of your choice, preferably clear. Add the flowers to the bottle until you achieve the desired look and fill.

Combine the essential oils, the oil from the vitamin E capsule and the coconut oil in a bowl and mix well. Pour the mixture into the bottle with the flowers, cap and shake gently. Allow the oil mixture to settle for a few moments, then add more oil if needed to fill the bottle. Use as you would a traditional body or bath oil to encourage patience and hope.

Restoring Hope Incense

This is probably my favorite incense of all time. Its energy is so sweet and supportive, just what you need during the waxing gibbous moon when you're almost at completion (the full moon) but feeling a little discouraged and perhaps ready to give up. Violets make this blend extra special. I think they embody the feeling of love and healing almost as much as rose does.

- 1 tbs copal resin
- 1 tbs dried blue sage
- 1 tbs dried rose petals
- 2 tsp dried juniper berries
- 1 tsp dried violets
- 1 tsp dried osmanthus
- 1 tsp dried hawthorn leaf and flowers

Mix all of the ingredients in a large bowl, then pour into an airtight container for storage. To use, light a charcoal incense disk until it begins to crackle and turn orange, then place it on a flameproof dish in a well-ventilated room. Sprinkle a pinch or two of incense onto the disk; it will begin to smoke as it burns. Allow the incense to continue to burn, adding another pinch if desired to reinvigorate the smoke.

Softness Diffuser Blend

I'll admit I am a worrier despite all of my spiritual training; must be my sun sign, Scorpio! I can also be quite restless and aggressive . . . Thanks, Mars in Aries! Needless to say, softness is something I always try to accomplish and usually fail at except when I have this diffuser blend filling my space. The fragrance has a very feminine, soft quality to it that makes it almost impossible to be worked up when you smell it. I also really like this blend for self-care days because it reminds me to slow down and remember that all things shall pass.

- 8 drops of geranium essential oil
- 6 drops of amyris essential oil
- 2 drops of angelica root essential oil
- 2 drops of rose absolute essential oil
- 1 drop of jasmine absolute essential oil

Combine the essential oils in a bottle with a dropper top if you are using one. Shake well to blend and store in a dark place out of direct sunlight. Add the blend to your aromatherapy diffuser, following the manufacturer's instructions.

CUCUMBER AND ALOE VERA CLEANSING WATER

I have extremely dry skin. On the one hand it means I've rarely had to fight acne, but on the other hand my skin is often flaky and itchy – at least, it was until I stopped using drying soaps made with harsh sulfates. I started making my own water-based cleanser, and it has worked miracles for my skin. Just be sure to wipe your face completely with a wipe before using this cleanser if you wear makeup during the day.

- ¼ cup Moon Water (page 27)
- ¼ cup aloe vera water
- ¼ cup cucumber hydrosol
- ¼ cup vegetable glycerin

- ¼ cup witch hazel
- 5 drops of palmarosa essential oil
- 5 drops of German chamomile essential oil

Combine all of the ingredients in a clean, sanitized squeeze bottle. Shake well before use. To use, squeeze a generous amount onto a cotton ball. Wipe one side of the cotton ball over your face and use the other side to gently dab over your eyes and wipe your lips. Rinse with warm water and follow with your favorite moisturizer.

REFRESHING INFUSED WATER

I believe beauty has a place in self-care and edible flowers make everything more beautiful, even boring water. Over the past couple of years I have found my spirits lift almost instantly when I spend a day basking in the simple pleasures of beautiful things such as this easy-to-make recipe that is upgraded with lemon and cucumber slices.

- rose quartz
- ½ cucumber, sliced
- 1 lemon, sliced
- 1–2 rosemary sprigs
- edible flowers

Add rose quartz, cucumber, lemon, and rosemary to a large, clear pitcher, then fill the pitcher with cool water. Place inside the refrigerator to infuse for several hours or overnight. Add the edible flowers to decorate then sip throughout the day for self-loving hydration.

Moon-Maker Tip: Make edible flower ice cubes ahead of time and keep them in the freezer instead of adding flowers to the pitcher.

Soul-Nourishing Morning Bath

A morning bath can feel quite indulgent, which is why I believe it is an excellent way to start a self-care day. You'll go into the rest of your morning feeling relaxed and, hopefully, ready to spend your entire day giving yourself some much needed pampering.

- 1 cup baking soda
- 1½ cups dry milk (see the Moon-Maker Tip on the next page)
- ¼ tsp mustard powder
- 1 grapefruit, sliced
- 8 drops of geranium essential oil
- 4 drops of jasmine absolute essential oil
- 1 drop of hyssop essential oil
- bouquet of carnations, optional
- white or cream candles, optional
- moonstone and clear quartz crystals, optional

Mix the baking soda, milk, mustard powder, grapefruit, and essential oils in a bowl with a whisk. Pour the mixture into an airtight container for storage and place it in a dark place such as a cabinet.

Fill your bathroom space with the carnations, candles, and crystals, putting as many as you can on or around the tub. Clear quartz can safely be added to the water if you desire. Light the candles and turn on soothing music if you like.

Run a warm bath that can be comfortably enjoyed for 20 to 30 minutes, then add a cup of the milk mixture and swirl it around with your hands just before stepping in. Relax in the bath, setting an intention for hope, patience, and peace of mind.

Moon-Maker Tip: There are different types of dry milk you can use, including coconut milk or oatmeal flour if you're not into using animal products. Otherwise, use whole fat, goat or buttermilk dry milk if you have dry skin, or nonfat dry milk if your skin is oily.

A QUIET WEEKEND AT HOME

I find cleaning to be a great way to take my mind off stressful things. I also find that my space is usually chaotic when I'm feeling as though I have too much on my plate, so when I'm not getting any forward movement I take a day to reset my mind, body, and home.

Below you will find my steps for resetting your energy, taking your mind away from anxiety and stressful events and packing in some holistic self-care.

Step 1: Make Refreshing Infused Water (page 113) the night before so it is cold.

Step 2: Put on uplifting, soothing, or energy-clearing music. (See Bonus Material, page 265, to access links to some of my favorite YouTube videos for background music.)

Step 3: Perfume your home by setting up an aromatherapy diffuser with your favorite essential oil blend; this book has plenty to choose from. Light candles and incense, and put on a simmer pot or give each room a spritz or two of your favorite ritual mist.

Step 4: Prep a Soul-Nourishing Morning Bath (page 115).

Step 5: Cleanse your face with the Cucumber and Aloe Vera Cleansing Water for dry skin (page 112) while running the bath.

Step 6: Lightly brush your skin using a dry brush, starting at your feet and working your way up and towards your heart. Next, brush your neck and shoulders, working again towards your heart.

Step 7: Lightly massage Patience Floral Bath and Body Oil (page 108) into your skin and step carefully into the tub. Soak for 20 minutes then towel off, leaving your skin slightly damp.

Step 8: Finish with a moisturizer, comfortable clothes and indoor shoes that are comfortable enough to be in all day.

MAKING NOURISHING MEALS

I call these kinds of meals "humble food." They are simple, clean, and nutrient packed, giving your body a break from denser foods. They're also pretty easy to make, so you don't have to waste a lot of time cooking.

SAVORY OATMEAL WITH GOAT CHEESE AND AVOCADO

This may sound like an unusual pairing, but it upgrades otherwise boring oatmeal and it is deliciously creamy and filling. It's also a great way to sneak in some protein and fat for a well-rounded meal, plus it's pretty good with a squeeze of lime on top. Combine these ingredients:

- 1 cup water
- ½ cup old-fashioned oatmeal
- 1 avocado, sliced or diced
- 1 oz | 30 g goat cheese
- salt and pepper to taste

Pineapple Cinnamon Smoothie

When I was a kid, my dad used to take me to a burger stand that served pineapple malt shakes. It was a truly decadent treat but it was packed full of sugar. Sadly, the burger joint isn't there anymore and my waistline is grateful, but every now and again I find myself missing the flavor. Therefore, I created a smoothie that is similar in taste but much more healthy. It's the perfect midday treat, uh hmm, lunch for a self-care day. Combine these ingredients in a blender:

- 1 cup diced pineapple
- ¼ cup pineapple juice
- ½ banana
- 1 tsp cinnamon root
- 1 cup oat milk
- 1 cup ice cube

Kale Salad with Strawberries, Pecans, and Grilled Steak

This is my go-to meal when I want something that is healthy, fresh, and substantial and still feels like a treat. Kale is infinitely better than lettuce in my opinion, and fresh strawberries bring a sweet, bright note. I love a simple grilled steak with salt, pepper, and butter. Of course, you can use something healthier like olive oil or margarine, but it won't quite taste as good.

VINAIGRETTE:

- ¼ cup balsamic vinegar
- 2 tbs honey
- 2 tsp Dijon mustard
- 1 garlic clove, minced
- salt and pepper to taste
- ¼ cup olive oil

STEAK:

- 4 oz | 120 g steak, New York strip or tenderloin
- salt and pepper to taste
- 2 tbs butter

SALAD:

- 1 bunch kale (I like lacinato kale)
- 1 tbs olive oil
- strawberries, sliced
- pecan halves
- Parmesan, shaved

Whisk together the vinaigrette ingredients except for the olive oil until well combined. Continue whisking while slowly drizzling in the olive oil. Taste and adjust the seasoning if needed. This dressing stores well in the refrigerator for several months. Keep it in a jar and shake well before each use.

Season both sides of the steak with salt and pepper. Melt half of the butter in a skillet over medium-low heat, then add the steak and cook for 5 minutes. Add the remaining butter, allowing it to melt, then spoon some of the butter over the top of the steak. Turn it over and cook on the other side. Spoon more of the butter on top and cook for another 5 minutes. Turn the steak up to high heat and cook until browned and the meat begins to form a crust, about 1 minute per side. Remove from the heat and allow the meat to rest on a plate for at least 10 minutes before slicing.

Chop the kale into large strips then massage with the olive oil to soften the leaves. Arrange the kale, strawberries, pecans, and Parmesan on a serving plate, add the steak on top and drizzle with the balsamic vinaigrette.

FOCUS ON THINGS THAT HAVE BEEN ON THE BACKBURNER

Sometimes the best thing you can do when you're lacking hope or haven't seen any progress is to take your mind off of things. A cluttered home is often a manifestation of a cluttered mind, and cleaning is a great way to keep busy while also tackling your to-do list. Don't be surprised to find your creative juices flowing after the end of a productive cleaning day. Try some of the following ways to clean or think up some other ways to keep your mind busy on your next quiet weekend:

- Wash clothes.
- Catch up on texts and emails from family and friends.
- Clean out the fridge and cabinets.
- Clean windows, window seals and screens, and picture frames while you're at it.
- Move furniture and vacuum, mop, or sweep underneath.
- Organize the junk drawers.
- Sort through old papers.
- Wash curtains, pillow cases, and blankets.
- Finish or start online courses you've already paid for or booked.
- Donate old clothes or things you haven't worn.
- Clean out weeds from the garden.
- Tackle small home repairs.

ENERGY CLEARING

Open as many doors and windows as you can to allow negative energy to escape, otherwise you'll just be pushing it around. To cleanse your space, start in the easternmost corner of your home and work clockwise. Be sure to always start in the east, the direction of new beginnings, when going from room to room.

As you spray or smudge, or work any method of your choice, be sure to tell spirit what it is you'd like them to do. You can ask to cleanse away negative energy and be provided with a safe and comforting environment, or you can ask for peace or vitality. Just be sure you're clear about your intention. Take some extra time in the spaces where the strange energy has occurred or any place that feels particularly stagnant. Work your way around each room, and be sure to thank spirit for cleansing and protecting your space before exiting. Continue until you've cleansed the entire house.

> *Moon-Maker Tip*: See page 132 for the Smoke-Clearing Bundle with Resin.

CHAPTER 9

FULL
MOON

The full moon is when, at least ideally, your new moon intentions have manifested. However, even if you didn't reach your goal just yet you can still use this time to celebrate what you have already done, whether that's acknowledging a few small but mighty steps or the success of a smaller goal in pursuit of a larger one. In this chapter I have included recipes for potions and food for bringing light to your accomplishments, because it's easy to overlook your achievements when you still have a laundry list of things to check off.

CLARITY

First and foremost, the full moon is about light. Use this time to bring awareness into how far you've come as well as gaining clarity about how far you have to go. If nothing else, use this newfound clarity to celebrate your progress, even if that's just one step forward. Any step in pursuit of your goals is a win in my opinion. Just be sure to share your success with others who love and care for you, which is why you'll find recipes and instructions in this chapter for throwing your own full moon gathering.

FULL MOON CORRESPONDENCES

Below is a list of ingredients and symbols that align with the energy of the full moon you can use as a starting point for creating your own lunar apothecary potions. Each ingredient has its own properties, bringing something unique to your magical potions. Be sure to check out correspondence tables in Appendix I to discover the individual characteristics of each ingredient.

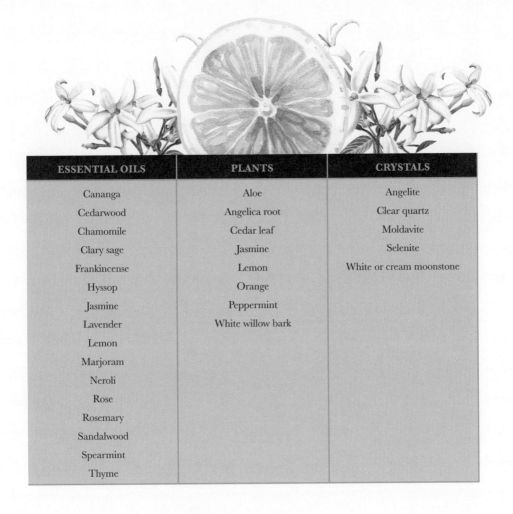

ESSENTIAL OILS	PLANTS	CRYSTALS
Cananga	Aloe	Angelite
Cedarwood	Angelica root	Clear quartz
Chamomile	Cedar leaf	Moldavite
Clary sage	Jasmine	Selenite
Frankincense	Lemon	White or cream moonstone
Hyssop	Orange	
Jasmine	Peppermint	
Lavender	White willow bark	
Lemon		
Marjoram		
Neroli		
Rose		
Rosemary		
Sandalwood		
Spearmint		
Thyme		

GRATEFUL GATHERING: THROWING A MOON PARTY TO CELEBRATE YOUR SUCCESS

In a perfect world, the intentions you set during the new moon will have come to fruition come the full moon, and what better way to celebrate than with your family and friends? Invite people over and ask them to bring their favorite crystals to charge with the energy of your success and gratitude as you dine under the moonlight. Follow these steps for a wonderful gathering.

Step 1: Invite your friends over and tell them to bring a few of their favorite crystals.

Step 2: To prepare for the party, make the Full Moon Spray for Clarity (page 131) and Moon Clearing and Charging Plate party favors (page 133). Find a nice space outdoors where you can set out chairs and a table that's big enough for you and your guests. Decorate the table using a tablecloth or fabric, florals, herbs, candles, and other items you enjoy, leaving space for platters of food. Lay out place settings for each guest and set out a party favor and bottle of spray for each place setting.

Step 3: Just before your guests arrive, light a Smoke-Clearing Bundle with Resin (page 132) and place it inside a terracotta pot that's close enough to your guests for them to smell it as the party moves on, but far enough away that the smoke doesn't become bothersome. Light additional bundles throughout the party if needed.

Arrange the Mozzarella, Yellow Tomato, and Purple Basil Salad, Citrus-Baked Halibut, Lemon Meringue Mini Tarts, and the preparations for the Moon Milk Cream Soda on the table among your decorations. Be sure to add smaller dishes of garnish, extra sauces, and salt and pepper for your guests, along with a stack of small gift bags so your guests can take their party favors home.

When your guests arrive, ask them to place their crystals on the charging dish next to their name. The crystals will charge with the energy of your celebration while you dine under the moon.

FULL MOON SPRAY FOR CLARITY

There are few ingredients that represent the moon more than jasmine, lemon, and rose, and they just happen to be a winning fragrance combination. Frankincense is also a great moon choice that adds a bit of depth and complexity to an otherwise simple blend.

- 4 oz | 120 ml Moon Water (page 27)
- 25 drops of jasmine absolute essential oil
- 50 drops of lemon essential oil
- a couple of drops of frankincense essential oil
- 1 tsp rose tincture or rose water

Fill a 4 oz | 120 ml bottle with all of the ingredients. Screw on a spray top and keep out of direct sunlight while storing. Allow the formula to synergize for at least one day, then shake well before each use and spray as desired. The spray will stay fresh for up to one year.

SMOKE-CLEARING BUNDLE WITH RESIN

This **DIY** bundle is similar to a traditional sage one but with resin hidden inside. I first made these as party favors, and they were a huge hit for my guests. Keep them all the same or change up the plant material and let your guests pick them intuitively, discovering the herb material they need most.

- fresh aromatic leaves such as sage
- 1–2 tsp herbs or plant sprigs per bundle (I used lavender and rosemary)
- resin (I used frankincense)
- twine

Gather up some aromatic herbs with large flat leaves such as sage or eucalyptus and allow them to dry out slightly. Lay the leaves flat on a surface to form a 3–4 in | 7.5–10 cm length of plant material with the long side facing toward you. Sprinkle the dried herbs and resin along the length of the leaves.

Roll the leaves, herbs, and resin into a bundle, starting at the long side and rolling into a tight jelly roll. Tie a length of the twine around the base, leaving a couple of inches loose. Wrap the loose twine around the entire length of the bundle, working up and then back down toward the base and pulling tightly to hold the contents in place.

Wrap the end of the twine a few times around the base, then tightly tie it to the beginning of the string. Tie the bundle up to dry out completely for a couple of weeks, then light as you would a traditional sage bundle.

Moon Clearing and Charging Plate

You can buy trinket dishes, of course, but making your own is so much more fun and allows you to customize the size, shape, and decoration. Make these up to use as party favors for the Grateful Gathering on page 130. Personalize each dish so your guests can see how much you love and appreciate their friendship.

- air-drying clay
- rolling pin
- small plate or bowl
- sharp knife
- paintbrush
- acrylic paint

Roll the clay into a large ball, then use the rolling pin to roll it out to about ¼ in | 6 mm thick. Lay the plate on top of the clay as a guide for cutting out a circle with the knife. Lay the plate on another section and cut out another circle, and repeat until you have enough circles.

Lay each circle on top of cups or bowls that are turned upside down to make bowl shapes, and allow them to dry overnight.

Paint the dishes as you please. You can also use stamps or decoupage cutouts of various designs.

Elderflower, Lemon, and Chamomile Simple Syrup

Elderflower and lemon is a winning combination, and chamomile is added for its correspondence to success, increased wealth, and peace. Use the syrup to flavor sparkling waters or in cocktails, or use it to make the Moon Milk Cream Soda recipe opposite.

- 1 tbs dried elderflower
- 1 lemon, sliced
- 1 tbs dried chamomile
- 1 cup sugar
- 1 cup water
- yellow food coloring, optional

Add all of the ingredients apart from the food coloring to a saucepan over medium heat, cooking just until the sugar dissolves. Remove from the heat and allow the syrup to steep and cool. Strain the herbs and lemon, then add food coloring if desired.

MOON MILK CREAM SODA

This recipe brings me so much joy. It combines two of my favorite drinks: an Italian-style cream soda with moon milk. I feel like maca powder makes everything taste creamier and I almost always add it to any kind of milk-based drink, so it seemed right at home here. Since no one wants to carry around warm moon milk at a party, I thought a soda would be the perfect way to uplift this soothing drink.

- 3 tbs Elderflower, Lemon, and Chamomile Simple Syrup opposite
- 8 oz | 240 ml lemon-flavored sparkling water
- 1 tsp maca powder
- 2 tbs half and half (see the Moon-Maker Tip on the next page for a vegan substitution)
- whipped cream

Fill glasses with ice cubes and the simple syrup, then top with enough sparkling water to reach about three-quarters of the way up the glass. In a separate container, blend the maca powder and half and half using a latte whisk. Pour the mixture into each glass. There is no need to stir it, as the half and half will float down throughout the entire drink. Top with the desired amount of whipped cream and sprinkle a bit more maca powder on top to garnish. Serve with paper straws and a long spoon.

I've also made this with great success using elderflower liqueur in place of the simple syrup.

Moon-Maker Tip: Substitute the half and half and whipped cream with coconut cream, or look for plant-based half and half and whipped cream in your local market. Silk half and half is my favorite vegan alternative for this recipe.

THE MOON MENU

MOZZARELLA, YELLOW TOMATO, AND PURPLE BASIL SALAD

This is an updated version of an old classic. Slices of mozzarella instantly remind you of full moons and feel right at home for a moon menu. Yellow tomatoes are my favorite, as I find them a bit brighter and fresher than red tomatoes – and, as a bonus, their color is reminiscent of moonlight.

- 2 cups white balsamic vinegar
- 1 tbs olive oil
- 12 oz | 340 g sliced mozzarella
- 3–4 whole large yellow tomatoes
- handful of purple basil, separated from the stems
- salt and pepper to taste

Bring the vinegar to the boil in a small saucepan, then reduce the heat to low and cook for 20 minutes. The liquid should be thicker and considerably reduced. Remove from the heat and allow the glaze to cool. When cooled, mix the glaze with the olive oil and set aside.

Arrange the mozzarella and tomato slices on a serving platter, then sprinkle the basil over the top. You can also put some between the layers of tomato and mozzarella. Pour the glaze and oil mixture evenly over the salad, then season with the salt and pepper. Serve and enjoy!

Citrus-Baked Halibut

This quick and easy recipe is perfect for an al fresco dinner party. It's fresh but still substantial, and requires very little prep work. I like to serve it with baked heirloom carrots and baby potatoes.

- 4 halibut filets
- dry white wine
- 2 tsp olive oil
- salt and pepper to taste
- 1 lemon, sliced
- 1 lime, sliced
- 1 orange, sliced

Preheat the oven to 400°F | 200°C.

Line a large baking pan with foil and spray the foil with cooking spray. Pour in some wine and arrange the halibut on top in a single layer. Drizzle the olive oil over the filets and season with salt and pepper.

Layer the citrus slices around the filets, then cover the pan with foil and bake for 15–20 minutes. Pour juices over the fish to serve.

LEMON MERINGUE MINI TARTS

I am not a big fruit or pie eater. I know, unpopular opinion, but it really isn't my thing. I do, however, love lemon meringue pie, and this one is extra special to me. It's my grandmother's recipe, and when my mom gave it to me after she passed I noticed how similar our handwriting was. In fact, it's so identical I thought at first I'd written it. It's also the only lemon-curd recipe I've been able to make, and there have been many recipes and many attempts. Since I'm manifesting becoming a spiritual lifestyle expert − ;-) − it makes me so sad to think my grandmother won't be able to join me if I ever have a TV show or a full-on cookbook, but at least I can share a little bit of her through her recipes.

- pie crust (homemade or store bought)
- 1 cup sugar + 6 tbs extra
- ¼ cup cornstarch
- dash of salt
- 1½ cups cold water
- 3 eggs, separated and room temperature
- ¼ cup lemon juice
- peel of 1 lemon, grated
- 1 tbs unsalted butter

Preheat the oven to 350°F | 180°C. Roll out the pie crust and cut out small circles using a round cookie or biscuit cutter. Place each circle inside the cavity of a cupcake tin and cover each one with a small piece of waxed paper. Put dry beans or rice on top and bake for 10–15 minutes. Remove from the oven and leave the shells to cool in the pan.

In a medium saucepan, combine the sugar, cornstarch, and salt. Gradually stir in the water, mixing until smooth. Bring to the boil over medium heat and cook, stirring constantly, until thick, about 5 minutes. Remove from the heat and stir a small amount of the mixture into the egg yolks, then pour the yolks into the remaining mixture in the saucepan. Bring to a boil, stirring constantly, and cook for about 1 minute. Remove from heat and add the lemon juice, lemon peel (reserving 1 teaspoon), and butter, and mix well until smooth. When the lemon curd is cool, spoon it into the baked pie shells.

Beat the egg whites with the reserved lemon peel in a stand mixer until soft peaks begin to form. Gradually add the extra sugar, beating until stiff peaks form and the sugar has dissolved. Gently add the meringue to a pastry bag and pipe it over the lemon curd in the tarts. Alternatively, spoon the mixture over top, spreading it to the edges of the crusts.

Bake for 12–15 minutes or until the meringue is a nice golden brown color. Remove from the oven and cool.

CHAPTER 10

WANING GIBBOUS MOON

The waning gibbous moon encourages acts of self-compassion, reflection, and gratitude. It's a wonderful time to evaluate your progress and reassess your goals. The recipes and rituals in this chapter will clear out any negative energy you might be experiencing from feelings of failure or slow progress, to relax your mind and body and, most importantly, to promote a feeling of self-love.

REFLECTION

A self-reflection practice is for the purpose of clarity, offering knowledge needed to formulate next steps rather than an excuse to put yourself down. It is a chance to open your mind so that you can learn from your successes and failures, putting that information to good use come the next moon cycle when it's time to set new intentions. It's also an opportunity to renew your spirit by checking in with what doesn't work and needs to be released.

WANING GIBBOUS MOON CORRESPONDENCES

Below is a list of ingredients and symbols that align with the energy of the waning gibbous moon you can use as a starting point for creating your own lunar apothecary potions. Each ingredient has its own properties, bringing something unique to your magical potions. Be sure to check out the correspondence tables in Appendix I to discover the individual characteristics of each ingredient.

ESSENTIAL OILS	PLANTS	CRYSTALS
Amyris	Moss	Amazonite
Eucalyptus	Orris root	Clear quartz
Fennel	Peppermint	Fluorite
Fir needle	Poppy seed	Jasper
Hyssop	Saffron	Lepidolite
Juniper	Star anise	
Marjoram		
Pine		
Rosemary		
Sage		
Thyme		
Valerian		

Self-Reflection Journaling Ritual

Here is a ritual that will relax you, clear your mind, and connect you with your inner self. After that has been done you can engage in journaling prompts that will help you make sense of your past, get to know your body better, and start to craft some goals for your future. It's the perfect ritual for the waning gibbous moon but, really, it's lovely at any time, especially when you're lacking clarity.

Step 1, Clarity and Reflection Bath: Start with a relaxing self-care treat to wash off the day and to welcome a feeling of calm. Find the recipe on page 155.

Step 2, Self-Reflection Moon Mylk: Brew up a soothing adaptogenic drink for a cup of comfort, and sip it throughout the journal writing process. Find the recipe on page 152.

Step 3, aroma: Infuse your space with a relaxing blend of essential oils made specifically for journaling that promote clarity, self-reflection, and peacefulness. Find the recipe on page 153.

Step 4, set the scene: Fill your ritual space with healing and prep the right tools to help you make the most of your self-reflection. Try these crystals to promote clarity:

- amazonite
- amethyst
- fluorite
- hematite
- quartz
- tourmaline.

I have a special diary that is reserved solely for reflection and taking notes on spiritual guidance. It is highly decorative using things that, for me, represent intuition, purpose, and hope for the future. I keep the notebook on my altar so it is close to hand after ceremonies or for rituals just like this one. Beside it is a special blue pen for intuition that I've wrapped in sari silk in shades of purple and blue. Having dedicated tools makes the entire process a bit more sacred and further helps to separate your spiritual life from your mundane one.

Candles make everything a bit more dreamy. I like to use them for ritual to set the tone of a calming environment and to add a little extra fragrance. The whole point of rituals is to make it a little bit of a special time that's devoted to you and your growth, so go all out with the luxury as much as you can.

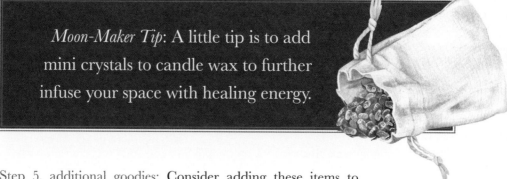

Moon-Maker Tip: A little tip is to add mini crystals to candle wax to further infuse your space with healing energy.

Step 5, additional goodies: Consider adding these items to further infuse your space and ritual practice with dreamy magic:

- Music: There is an endless supply of music on YouTube for raising vibrations, promoting peace, cleansing the aura, and pretty much every intention you can think of. See Bonus Material, page 265, to check out some of my favorites.

- Plants: Even houseplants have healing properties, and if nothing else they help to keep air free. Try out different plants to see which ones you like best. My favorite is fiddle leaf.

- Breath exercises: Conscious breathing using specific exercises can help to reduce anxiety, balance your brain, and encourage better focus.

- Comfortable clothing: You want to feel completely unrestricted and relaxed. Choose your favorite lounge clothes or dedicate something special for ritual purposes.

- No tech: do this with an analog pen and paper so you don't have any distractions. Also, turn off your notifications.

Step 6, a container for self-reflection: Prior to journaling, do this exercise to energetically separate your ritual space from the mundane.

A Container for Self-Reflection: Before engaging in this meditative, ritual work it's important to create a separation between your mundane life and your spiritual practice. There are a few ways you can do this, but my favorite is by visualizing a container or light around you. This practice is like leaving your worries at the door. Once inside, your mind should be clear and focused on you, giving you the space needed to reflect.

First, close your eyes and imagine all of your anxieties and worries sitting inside a box. Visualize throwing that box away from you without worrying where it lands. With your eyes still closed, create the light by visualizing a bubble of light emanating from your heart space and encircling you. Inside the bubble there is a beautiful, warm glow that is soothing and calming. The outside of the bubble has a mirror that reflects and sends any unwanted energy back to its place of origin. If any of the worries from that box try to reach you, they too will bounce off the mirror.

Step 7, say a prayer for guidance (see page 150).

Step 8, self-love letters: **Journal** prompts guide you through getting to know yourself and your journey with more clarity and understanding. The self-love letters are journaling prompts that are designed to help you separate your true self from the parts of you that feel broken, depleted, or unmotivated so you can think clearly and from a place that intuitively knows what to do and how to think. This place, your inner self, is what you should be tapping into when you think about your hopes, dreams, needs, and desires. You don't have to do these letters all at once, and I don't recommend it. A lot can come up during these writing sessions, and having time to process between them keeps it from being so overwhelming.

Write a letter to your past: Which part of your past you write to is up to you, but here are some suggestions. You can write a letter to your 20-year-old self and talk about all of the things you wish you knew then. You can write a letter to a version of yourself that you don't really like, perhaps someone who wasn't focused in school or who went through a period of going out and drinking too much. Don't censor yourself, but also have some compassion. Ultimately, write to the past you and tell them all of the things you wish someone had told you then. Be that person you needed in your life at that time and support the part that is waiting for a helping hand.

Write a letter to your body: Write a letter to your body about how you feel toward it. It can be positive or negative, as long as it's honest. Some ideas could be an apology for how you might've mistreated or neglected your body. You can write a letter of love and talk about the things you like about your body. You can also write a letter of commitment and explain what you'll do to show up more for your body's self-care.

Write a letter from your future self to you: Describe all of the things you've accomplished, people you've met, new relationships, old relationships that have developed, and places you've been. Talk about the home you live in or the way you dress. You can even talk about how you feel and how your personality has changed over time.

Write a letter to your future self: In this letter, talk about your values and beliefs. This letter is for you to check back in with your core values, to remind your future self of things that are important to remember. For example, if you're starting a business you'll write to your future self as a CEO of a Fortune 500 company. Consider writing about the reasons you started the company, what you hope to accomplish, and who you're doing this for. Write about the feelings of making your first sale or getting your first contract. When you're finished with this letter, sign and date it, then put it somewhere you'll regularly see it. Read it when you need to be reminded of who you are.

Step 9, say a prayer for closing your ritual (see page 151).

Step 10, close your eyes and visualize the light being drawn back into your heart space. You can also use this technique if ever you're feeling vulnerable, need some personal space, or wish to energetically protect yourself from others.

GUIDANCE PRAYER

Say this before journaling:

*Higher self, I humbly request the courage, love,
and wisdom needed to get to know myself and
my journey in all my glory. I will do my best to
honor the guidance flowing through me today.*

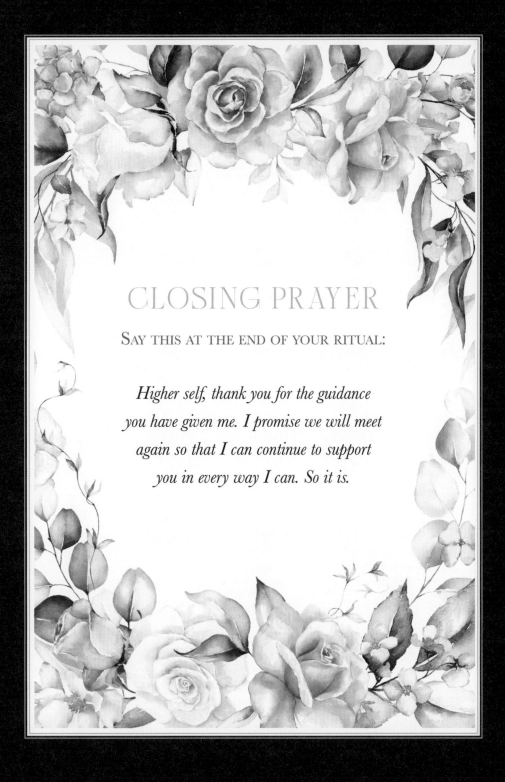

CLOSING PRAYER

Say this at the end of your ritual:

*Higher self, thank you for the guidance
you have given me. I promise we will meet
again so that I can continue to support
you in every way I can. So it is.*

Self-Reflection Moon Mylk

This is one of my favorite calming drinks – not just for journaling, but any time I want to foster a sense of peace. Moringa and mucuna inspire spiritual well-being and high-vibrational bliss, while lion's mane is excellent for memory, concentration, and helping to reduce stress.

- 1 tsp moringa powder
- ½ tsp lion's mane powder
- ½ tsp maca powder
- ½ tsp mucuna powder
- 2 tbs warm water
- 8 oz | 240 ml almond milk or other plant-based milk
- 1 tbs coconut butter
- coconut sugar to taste

Whisk the moringa, lion's mane, maca, and mucuna powders into the water. Gently warm the milk in a saucepan; do not allow the milk to boil. When the milk is warm, add in the coconut butter to melt. Remove from the heat and gently whisk into the moringa mixture, along with the coconut sugar. Pour into your favorite mug and sip while journaling.

Journaling Essential Oil Blend

Keep the vibration of your space clear with this essential oil blend, made specifically to encourage self-reflection and clarity. Set up your diffuser with the recipe any time you are reviewing your progress and goals.

- 8 drops of frankincense essential oil
- 5 drops of clary sage essential oil
- 8 drops of marjoram essential oil
- 19 drops of mandarin essential oil

Pour the oils into a bottle with a dropper top if you are using one. Shake well to blend and store in a dark place out of direct sunlight. Add the blend to your aromatherapy diffuser following the manufacturer's instructions.

CLARITY AND REFLECTION CORDIAL

This bath cordial will help you to relax, clear negative energy, and promote a better understanding of yourself and your circumstances. Reflecting on your recent successes or failures is best done when you are at ease, so you can view yourself through a compassionate but honest lens.

- 3–4 rosemary sprigs
- 2 star anise pods
- 4 cloves
- 1 cup brandy or rum
- 2 tsp glycerin
- 2 tbs unscented Castile soap
- 2 tsp Virginian cedarwood essential oil
- 1 tsp pine essential oil

Slip the rosemary sprigs, star anise pods, and cloves into an 8 oz | 240 ml bottle. You may need to break up the star anise to fit it through the neck. Mix the brandy, glycerin, soap, and essential oils together, then pour into the bottle. Cap tightly and shake gently, then place in a cool, dark place for three to four days, shaking periodically. This mixture can be used on its own or in the following recipe. To use, add 1 tablespoon to a warm bath and swish around to distribute.

CLARITY AND REFLECTION BATH

- 2 tbs fresh thyme
- 2 cups milk powder (or coconut milk for a vegan option)
- 1 tbs Clarity and Reflection Cordial (opposite)

Bring 4 cups of water to a boil then remove from the heat. Add the thyme, cover, and steep for 20 minutes. Strain the thyme from the mixture into a bowl, then add the milk powder and the Clarity and Reflection Cordial.

Draw a bath, adjusting to a comfortable temperature. Add the milk mixture to the bath and get in. Submerge yourself in the bath and relax for 20 to 30 minutes. While soaking, take a few moments to inhale the scent and imagine the fragrance moving through your body, clearing out any stagnant energy.

After your bath, towel dry and moisturize, then if you like proceed to the Self-Reflection Journaling Ritual (see page 145).

CHAPTER 11

LAST QUARTER MOON

The last quarter moon is luna's way of encouraging you to confront your baggage so you can finally let it go, making space for new things to come at the next new moon. This is one of the more difficult moon phases to manage as it requires a great deal of truth, courage, and a willingness to change for your greater good. In this chapter you will find a selection of potions for energetically releasing your blocks, but I have also included grounding recipes to help you manage the feelings of grief that are often associated with having to let things go.

RELEASING

No one's journey is without sacrifice. There will be times when someone, something, or even your most exciting dreams get in the way of your growth. That doesn't mean anything is wrong with them or you, or that you've made the wrong choices. It simply comes down to outgrowing who you were and trying on who you're becoming. That can mean releasing toxic attachments and behaviors, but it can also mean shedding one goal in favor of another or just shaking off an especially difficult day. Try not to see "releasing" solely in good or bad terms or that it has to be something physical. There are many ways to shed old layers of energy.

Unsure of what needs to be released? Check out Chapter 10, Waning Gibbous Moon for a self-reflection ritual.

GROUNDING

It takes a lot of energy to release things. There is the emotion of having to confront and acknowledge the thing that needs to go, as well as the grief associated with the vacancy in your life. The last quarter moon can stimulate some challenging feelings and deplete your vitality, which is why grounding is so important during this phase. Grounding, or what is sometimes called "rooting" or "centering," is a way to anchor your energy, giving you something to hold on to when the world around you is spinning in chaos. It's something comfortable you can rely on without worrying about it slipping through your fingertips.

Rituals are naturally grounding, but you can make them even more centering by focusing on ingredients that strengthen your spirit, encouraging feelings of stability and support.

LAST QUARTER MOON CORRESPONDENCES

Below is a list of ingredients and symbols that align with the energy of the last quarter moon you can use as a starting point for creating your own lunar apothecary potions. Each ingredient has its own properties, bringing something unique to your magical potions. Be sure to check out correspondence tables in Appendix I to discover the individual characteristics of each ingredient.

ESSENTIAL OILS	PLANTS	CRYSTALS
Benzoin	Angelica root	Amethyst
Cedarwood	Barley	Aquamarine
Clove	Coffee	Black tourmaline
Cypress	Patchouli	Hematite
Fir needle	Pine needles	Smoky quartz
Ginger	Sage	Yellow fluorite
Juniper	Sea salt	
Lavender	Tarragon	
Patchouli		
Rosemary		
Sage		
Sandalwood		
Spearmint		
Spruce		
Tea tree		
Thyme		

Release Incense-Burning Ritual

The last quarter phase of the moon is an excellent time to let go of things that are no longer in alignment with your life story. This ritual offers release in two ways. First, you'll burn what no longer serves, and then you'll gently scrub and wash it away. Visualization is a wonderful tool, but the physical act of shedding dead skin from your body makes spiritual release feel more tangible and real, especially when you're attempting to shed something that has held you back for a long time. Think of it as throwing away mementos after a breakup: seeing something physically leave gives you a feeling of resetting so you can move on.

Repeat this ritual as many times as needed during the last quarter moon phase, until you feel you have fully released what you no longer wish to carry. For this ritual you will need:

- Releasing Incense Blend (page 162)
- Releasing Body Scrub (page 164)
- Grounding Body Cream (page 168)
- Grounding Spray (page 165)

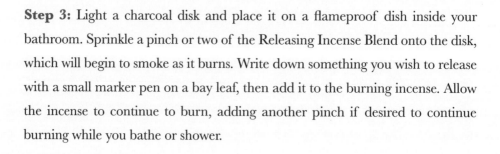

Step 1: Prepare all of the recipes needed for this ritual.

Step 2: Run a warm bath or prepare a warm shower.

Step 3: Light a charcoal disk and place it on a flameproof dish inside your bathroom. Sprinkle a pinch or two of the Releasing Incense Blend onto the disk, which will begin to smoke as it burns. Write down something you wish to release with a small marker pen on a bay leaf, then add it to the burning incense. Allow the incense to continue to burn, adding another pinch if desired to continue burning while you bathe or shower.

Step 4: Think about what you wrote down on the bay leaf. Notice any areas of your body that feel tight or offer a sensation when you bring this thing to mind.

Step 5: Massage the Releasing Body Scrub all over your body, focusing on the areas where you felt a sensation while thinking about what you wish to release.

Step 6: Rinse off the body scrub, taking as long as you like to let the warm water relax and soothe you.

Step 7: Towel dry, leaving just a little bit of moisture on the skin. Massage the Grounding Body Cream all over your body, spending extra time on your lower body and especially your feet.

Step 8: You may feel a little drained or tired after this releasing ritual, especially if what you've released was something significant or has been a part of your story for a long time. Use the Grounding Spray over the next few days, misting your space lightly whenever you feel unsteady.

> *Moon-Maker Tip:* Don't limit yourself to things that feel negative. You may choose to release an outdated goal to make space for a new one, release the attachment to a home when you're moving, or even say goodbye to a loved one who has passed on, offering up your hopes and prayers for their next journey.

Releasing Incense Blend

It's said your wish will come true if you write it on a bay leaf and burn it. A desire to release something is also a wish, and this practice is easily adapted to banish something from your life.

- 2 tbs dragon's blood resin
- 1 tbs ground coffee powder
- 1 tbs dried chamomile flowers
- 2 tsp dried sage leaf
- 1 tsp dried horehound
- 1 tsp dried patchouli leaf
- 1 tsp dried angelica root
- bay leaves

Mix all of the ingredients except the bay leaves in a large bowl, then pour into an airtight container for storage. To use, light a charcoal incense disk until it begins to crackle and turn orange, then place it on a flameproof dish in a well-ventilated room. Sprinkle a pinch or two of incense mixture onto the disk. It will begin to smoke as it burns.

Write down something you'd like to release on the surface of a bay leaf. It doesn't need to be a lot: you can just write down a word or even a symbol that represents what you're banishing. Add the bay leaf to the charcoal disk to burn along with the incense mixture and watch as what you have written burns away. Allow the incense to continue to burn, adding another pinch of the mixture if desired to reinvigorate the smoke.

Dragon's Blood–Infused Marjoram Essential Oil

One of my favorite blends to make is to steep ingredients in essential oils, the same way you would steep plants in alcohol to make a tincture. Really aromatic plant material such as resins, vanilla beans, spices, and even fresh flowers bring a wonderful complexity to essential oils and can be a great way to make use of an ingredient that might be too expensive to purchase in essential oil form or one that is not available as an oil.

- 1 tsp dragon's blood resin
- ¼ cup marjoram essential oil
- 1 tsp vodka, optional but recommended

Combine all of the ingredients in a small bowl or bottle with a lid and allow the mixture to steep overnight. Strain the mixture and pour the liquid into a dark glass-dropper bottle and label accordingly. Allow the dragon's blood resin to dry on a piece of parchment to use for incense; you don't have to throw it away.

Releasing Body Scrub

A body scrub dedicated to something intangible you'd like to let go of is one of the best ways to incorporate the energy of releasing into your everyday self-care. This scrub is an all-purpose base for releasing any intention. Simply bring to mind what you are ready to let go of before using it, and imagine you are gently scrubbing away what no longer serves as you massage it around your body.

- ¾ cup coconut sugar
- ¼ cup salt
- 9 drops of Dragon's Blood–Infused Marjoram Essential Oil (see page 163)
- 1 tsp finely ground black tea leaves
- 1 tsp vanilla extract
- ½ cup grapeseed oil

In a bowl, vigorously whisk the sugar and salt with the infused essential oil, then blend in the remaining ingredients. Spoon the mixture into a container with a tight lid. To apply, massage a small amount onto moist skin, rubbing in a counterclockwise motion, then rinse. Use within six to eight months. Refrigeration is not required.

GROUNDING SPRAY

Releasing is a necessary part of a spiritual journey, but it can take a lot of energy to finally let go of things you've been holding on to for a long time. This grounding spray will help you stabilize yourself after release rituals, or any time you feel disoriented, off balance, or as though you're floating through life rather than being present. You will need to make a tincture for this spray ahead of time because it takes about two to four weeks, but once the tincture is made you should have plenty to make this spray again and again.

FOR THE TINCTURE:

- green tea or coffee grounds
- 8 oz | 240 ml jar with a tight-fighting lid
- vodka
- wax paper
- cheesecloth or coffee filters
- amber-colored bottle

FOR THE SPRAY:

- garnet chips
- 8 drops of clary sage essential oil
- 11 drops of blue cypress essential oil
- 12 drops of jasmine absolute essential oil
- 19 drops of Spanish sage essential oil
- 7 oz | 200 ml distilled water

To make the tincture, fill the jar with the green tea or coffee grounds, leaving about 1 in | 2.5 cm of room at the top. Cover the plant material with the vodka, still leaving space at the top. Put the wax paper over the mouth of the jar, then screw on the lid. Shake the jar to distribute the contents evenly, adding more vodka if needed to cover the plant material.

Label the jar with the name and date, and place it somewhere dark. Shake the jar every day for two to four weeks. The longer it sits, the more potent it will be. Strain the plant material through cheesecloth or a coffee filter, pressing out as much of the oil as possible. Compost the plant material. Store the tincture in the amber bottle, name and date it, and store it in a dark, cool place.

To make the spray, add a handful of garnet chips to a spray bottle then fill with the essential oils, water, and 2 teaspoons of the tincture. Screw on a spray top and keep out of direct sunlight while storing. Allow the formula to synergize for at least one day, then shake well before each use and spray as desired. The spray will stay fresh for up to one year.

Moon-Maker Tip: Garnet is sometimes called the "crisis" stone for its ability to encourage harmony and strength through difficult times, as well as renew hope, courage, and a sense of calm.

GROUNDING BODY CREAM

Making emulsified body creams feels intimidating at first, but they are a lot of fun with a little bit of practice and they offer a lots of opportunities to customize many layers of the potion. Switch up the water, infuse the oils with different plant materials and, of course, play around with the scents.

- ½ cup aloe vera water
- 1 tsp vegetable glycerin
- ¼ cup Basic Oil Infusion (see page 168) using sage and coconut oil
- 2 tsp stearic acid
- 1 tbs emulsifying wax
- 1 tsp vitamin E oil
- 40 drops of Virginia cedarwood essential oil
- 20 drops of rosemary essential oil

Pour the water into a glass measuring cup and place the cup inside a saucepan that contains several inches of water. Simmer until the temperature measures 160°F | 70°C, then immediately remove from the heat and stir in glycerin.

Combine the infused oil, acid, and wax in a separate glass measuring cup and place inside a saucepan that contains several inches of water. Simmer until the temperature measures 160°F | 70°C, then immediately remove from heat. Both mixtures need to stay within three to four degrees of each other once removed from the heat.

Pour the oil mixture into a heatproof bowl and begin mixing with a hand mixer. Slowly add the water mixture and continue to mix until it cools to 118°F | 48°C. Add the vitamin E oil and essential oils and mix well. Transfer the cream to a clean glass jar and store in the refrigerator for up to 15 days.

CHAPTER 12

WANING CRESCENT MOON

Τ he waning crescent moon is your last chance to reset your energy before the moon cycle starts again with the new moon and things start to pick up. Passive periods are necessary to give your spirit a break between the hustle and bustle of setting intentions and working your plan of attack.

REST

Resting periods help to reduce any pressure you might feel to see results. It can be really easy to get caught up in a need to set intentions all the time or to jump from one goal to another without taking it break. It can be just as frustrating trying to seek spiritual guidance and feeling like you aren't getting anywhere. Taking care of yourself is just as valuable as connecting with your spirit guides, working rituals, or setting intentions, so I like to use this period to do nothing but focus on self-care.

WANING CRESCENT MOON CORRESPONDENCES

Below is a list of ingredients and symbols that align with the energy of the waning crescent moon you can use as a starting point for creating your own lunar apothecary potions. Each ingredient has its own properties, bringing something unique to your magical potions. Be sure to check out correspondence tables in Appendix I to discover the individual characteristics of each ingredient.

ESSENTIAL OILS	PLANTS	CRYSTALS
Bergamot	Calendula	Amethyst
Caraway	Carnation	Bloodstone
Cypress	Horehound	Blue calcite
Frankincense	Lavender	Howlite
Juniper	Lily	Lepidolite
Lavender	Olive leaf	Sodalite
Lemon balm	Orange	
Marjoram	Thyme	
Nutmeg		
Orange		
Petitgrain		
Rosemary		
Spruce		

Nourishing Night-In Ritual

I started doing this night-time ritual in 2022 when I was experiencing a very difficult time of release that was necessary for me to welcome in much new growth. It took a lot of energy out of me all the same, and I found myself stressing at night when I was going to bed and I wasn't waking up feeling rested. I created this ritual to help calm my mind and ease me into a gentle sleep. The key is dedicating time to doing the ritual. At first, you may want to do other things – I know I did – but this act of self-care was so essential in helping me find a better quality of sleep. On top of that, I found myself experiencing less stress throughout the day and felt much more prepared when things started moving forward again.

- Warm Eye Poultice (page 177)

- candles of your choice

- Me-Time Diffuser Blend (page 176)

- shallow dish

- ice cubes

- clean washcloth

- Calming Night Lotion (page 179)

Step 1: Brew tea for the eye poultice in the morning and allow it to cool. Store it in the refrigerator until you are ready to use it.

Step 2: Set the mood by lighting candles and dimming and turning off the lights. Fill an aromatherapy diffuser with the Me-Time Diffuser Blend, place it somewhere nearby, and turn it on continuous mode. Put on relaxing music. See Bonus Material, page 265, to gain access to my Me-Time Spotify playlist.

Step 3: Pour the eye poultice into the dish with a few ice cubes to keep the mixture cold. Fold a washcloth into thirds lengthwise and place it into the tea until it is fully saturated. Sit in a comfortable place or lie down if you prefer. Set a timer for 20 minutes. Wring out the washcloth and place it over your eyes, pressing the cloth gently around the eye area to create a blanket-like feel. Relax with the cloth over your eyes until the timer goes off. You can dip the cloth into the tea again as needed if it becomes too warm. Discard the tea once the timer goes off.

Step 4: Do the following stretches while sitting on top of your bed:

- happy baby
- butterfly
- upside down legs
- ankle stretches
- hamstring stretches
- knees to chest
- shoulder lift and release
- child's pose.

Step 5: Massage the Calming Night Lotion into your feet, hands, chest, and neck. Bring your hands to your nose and inhale three times, then slip into the covers.

Step 6: Goodnight, and rest well!

Me-Time Diffuser Blend

I believe self-care should incorporate all of the senses, but especially smell, because a great-smelling space goes a long way towards fostering peace of mind. I'll put on my aromatherapy diffusers all day when I'm at home and sometimes in my Spirit Element warehouse as well, and my heart fills with a little moment of joy every time I catch a whiff of fragrance in the air. I love to experience a different fragrance, sometimes a new one every day, but the Me-Time Diffuser Blend is one of my go-to favorites for slow days.

- 5 drops of Roman chamomile essential oil
- 31 drops of bergamot essential oil
- 14 drops of frankincense essential oil
- rhodochrosite chips, optional

Pour the essential oils and rhodochrosite chips into a bottle with a dropper top if you are using one. Shake well to blend and store in a dark place out of direct sunlight. Add the blend to your aromatherapy diffuser, following the manufacturer's instructions.

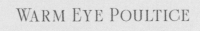

Warm Eye Poultice

Tired eyes can make you feel more tired than you actually are. We often overlook our eyes in terms of self-care, but you will be amazed how much better you feel once you give your eyes some TLC. This eye poultice feels so good on both dry and itchy eyes. I find the cool temperature and mint also help to reduce dark eyes and bags when used regularly.

- 1 tbs dried chamomile
- 1 tbs dried lavender
- 1 tbs dried peppermint
- green teabag
- 12 oz | 360 ml water
- 36 drops of lavender essential oil
- 8 drops of clary sage essential oil
- 6 drops of geranium essential oil
- 2 drops of Virginian cedarwood essential oil

Add the herbs and teabag to a heatproof bowl. Boil the water, then pour it over the herb mixture and allow it to steep for 20 minutes. Strain the mixture and compost the herbs. Allow the tea to cool, then pour it into a bottle and store it in the refrigerator to keep it cold until you're ready to use, or for at least two hours.

Add the essential oils to a dropper bottle and shake to mix well. This mixture will make enough for about 50 uses.

Pour the eye poultice tea into a shallow dish with two drops of the essential oil mixture and a few ice cubes to keep the mixture cold. Fold a washcloth into thirds lengthwise and place it into the tea until it is fully saturated. Wring out the washcloth and place it over your eyes, pressing the cloth gently around the eye area to create a blanket-like feel. Relax with the cloth over your eyes for about 20 minutes, or as long as you wish. You can dip the cloth into the tea again as needed if it becomes too warm. Discard the tea when you are finished.

Moon-Maker Tip: Freeze some of the eye poultice into ice cubes so it melts into your tea during your ritual without further diluting it with regular water.

CALMING NIGHT LOTION

This may sound silly, but I cannot sleep with dry hands or feet. I cannot stand it, so I always have a body lotion on my bedside table. Next to the lotion is my diffuser blend, which I fill with a calming night-time blend to help me sleep. Eventually, I added the same fragrance to an unscented lotion to rub on my skin before bed. I can smell the lotion on my hands while lying down and it has worked wonders, helping me to fall asleep more quickly. Give this lotion a try if you have a hard time quieting your mind at night.

- 16 oz | 480 ml unscented lotion
- 25 drops of lavender essential oil
- 15 drops of Roman chamomile essential oil
- 4 drops of vetiver essential oil

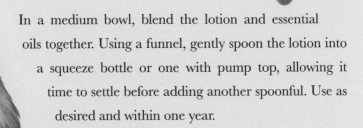

In a medium bowl, blend the lotion and essential oils together. Using a funnel, gently spoon the lotion into a squeeze bottle or one with pump top, allowing it time to settle before adding another spoonful. Use as desired and within one year.

CHAPTER 13

ECLIPSES

Lunar and solar eclipses are a marvel to witness, disrupting our normal view of the sun and moon with a stunning display. Spiritually, the energy of eclipses can manifest in swift and dramatic change, the ending of an era, and dealing with the rocky roads that often come with transitions. Generally, these changes are in your best interest, but that doesn't mean they are pleasant to experience. In this chapter you will find a selection of grounding, supportive potions that will also help you learn the lessons associated with lunar and solar eclipses.

LUNAR ECLIPSES: A CHANGE IN PERSPECTIVE

A lunar eclipse can only occur during a full moon when the earth is aligned between the sun and the moon. This heightened energy brings about dramatic change, the kind that may throw you off balance or force you to deal with a situation you've been avoiding. The effects of a lunar eclipse probably won't be pleasant, but it generally means the end of something that was blocking you from reaching higher levels of success. This cycle is meant to change your perspective, encouraging you to get out of your comfort zone and understand there is a new, better way for you to achieve your desires.

Nevertheless, change is hard to manage and accept. The recipes that follow will support you during intense and swift transitions that are likely out of your control. Often in the midst of change you will have to adapt to whatever is being thrown at you, which will likely require a lot of your strength and energy. These recipes in this chapter are focused on renewal, rebuilding hope, and finding clarity for what's to come.

LUNAR ECLIPSE CORRESPONDENCES

Below is a list of ingredients and symbols that align with the energy of lunar eclipses you can use as a starting point for creating your own lunar eclipse apothecary potions. Each ingredient has its own properties, bringing something unique to your magical potions. Be sure to check out correspondence tables in Appendix I to discover the individual characteristics of each ingredient.

ESSENTIAL OILS	PLANTS	CRYSTALS
Caraway	Marjoram	Hematite
Catnip	Peppermint	Moonstone
Clary sage	Sage	Red jasper
Coriander	Thyme	Red quartz
Cumin	Violet	Serpentine
Cypress	Witch hazel	
Fennel		
Fir needle		
Hemlock spruce		
Hyssop		
Mugwort		
Parsley		
Patchouli		
Peppermint		
Sage		
Tea tree		
Ylang ylang		

Shower Ritual for Everyday Stress Relief During Tough Times

The shower is a great place to decompress. You're already alone, so why not use this opportunity to cry when no one's watching and let yourself experience what you're feeling without worry of judgment? The recipes in this chapter and used for this ritual are all made to hold and support you while you're dealing with stressful times. Their sole function is to help you gently release any tension or heavy emotions you might be feeling. This ritual is wonderful for day or night, and there is no limit to how many times you need to use it no matter the moon phase.

- Diffuser Blends for Tough Times (page 187)
- Refreshing Shower Tablets (page 189)
- Support and Strength Shampoo (page 190)
- Held Conditioner (page 191)
- Held Body Wash (page 192)

Step 1: Put on an aromatherapy diffuser filled with one of the diffuser blends and place it somewhere in your home where you plan to spend the most time for the day, so you can smell the aroma once you leave the bathroom. Play music to set a calming environment for after your shower. (See Bonus Material, page 265, to gain access to a Spotify playlist for tough times.)

Step 2: Step into the shower and place one or two of the shower tablets on the floor, where the warm water will hit and dissolve it. Take a few moments to breathe in the aroma.

Step 3: Wash and conditioner your hair using the shampoo and conditioner, allowing the conditioner to stay in your hair for about 10 minutes.

Step 4: Wash your body using the body wash while your hair is conditioning, then rinse off from head to toe.

Step 5: Cry if you need to! Go ahead and let it all out while no one is watching.

Step 6: While still in the shower, or after drying off if you prefer, take three big cleansing breaths to revive after purging your emotions.

THYME TINCTURE

Thyme is one of those herbs that is overlooked as a kitchen ingredient and doesn't get enough of a voice in magic, at least in my opinion. This is a shame, because aside from being a great option for purification it's also very supportive for dealing with grief, attracting well-being, and facilitating peace.

- 8 oz | 240 ml jar with a tight-fighting lid
- several fresh thyme sprigs
- vodka
- waxed paper
- cheesecloth or coffee filters
- amber-colored dropper bottle

Fill the jar with thyme sprigs then cover with the vodka, leaving just a little room at the top. Put the waxed paper over the mouth of the jar and screw on the lid. Shake the jar to distribute the contents evenly, adding more alcohol if needed to cover the plant material.

Label the jar with the name and date and place it in a darkened place. Shake the jar every day for two to four weeks. The longer it sits, the more potent it will be.

Strain the liquid from the thyme through the cheesecloth or coffee filters and toss the thyme into the compost bin. Pour the tincture into the amber-colored bottle and label. Use this mixture for the Support and Strength Shampoo (page 190) and the Held Body Wash (page 192).

Diffuser Blends for Tough Times

The essential oil blends below are perfect for going through what I like to call the "spiritual desert," a time when you're feeling lost, confused, or cut off from spiritual guidance. They will help ease you through the ride of challenge, change, and chaos or just offer you some energetic support when you feel like you're carrying more than you can handle. Each blend has a specific energetic purpose, but all of them have a grounding and nourishing element to them in addition to encouraging clarity for what's to come.

PEACE AND STRENGTH ESSENTIAL OIL BLEND

- 10 drops of Dalmatian sage essential oil
- 6 drops of rosemary essential oil
- 3 drops of star anise essential oil

OVERCOMING CHALLENGES ESSENTIAL OIL BLEND

- 7 drops of Roman Chamomile essential oil
- 11 drops of lavender essential oil
- 3 drops of hemlock spruce essential oil

EMOTIONAL RELEASE ESSENTIAL OIL BLEND

- 9 drops of cedarwood atlas essential oil
- 9 drops of palmarosa essential oil
- 4 drops of rosemary essential oil

CLEAR SORROW FROM THE MIND, BODY AND SOUL ESSENTIAL OIL BLEND

- 9 drops of clary sage essential oil

- 7 drops of hyssop essential oil

- 2 drops of myrtle essential oil

- 11 drops of lavender essential oil

Refreshing Shower Tablets

These tablets are the perfect way to introduce scent and invigoration to an otherwise boring shower. They are simple to make and, like pretty much everything in this book, can easily be customized by switching out the herb material and essential oils.

- 1 cup baking soda
- 1 tsp dried herb powder (I use marjoram powder)
- ¼ cup water
- silicone molds with small cavities
- essential oil blend of your choice (I use the Peace and Strength Essential Oil Blend above)

Mix the baking soda, herb powder, and water together in a bowl until well combined. Spoon equal amounts of the mixture into each cavity of the molds and press firmly to smooth the tops. Bake in a 350°F | 180°C oven for about 15 minutes or until hard. Remove from the molds and allow the shapes to cool and dry on a plate.

Add three to four drops of the essential oil to each shape and again allow them to dry. Store in an airtight container. To use, place one or two tablets on the floor of a warm shower, inhale and enjoy the fragrance.

SUPPORT AND STRENGTH SHAMPOO

Thyme and blessed thistle are beautiful herbs for processing heavy emotions such grief or just dealing with the inevitable ebbs and flow of life's journey. All change, even good change, can be a real challenge. Switch out your normal shampoo for this one when you're experiencing a cycle of swift, dramatic changes and transitions. It will help to support you and infuse your spirit with the strength and courage you need to get through anything you're facing.

- 2 cups distilled water
- 3 tbs fresh sage leaves
- 1 tbs dried blessed thistle
- 1 tsp Thyme Tincture (page 185)
- ½ cup mint-scented Castile soap
- 20 drops of essential oil

Bring the water to the boil in a medium-sized saucepan, then remove from heat. Add the sage and blessed thistle, cover with a towel and allow it to steep until completely cooled. Strain the liquid into a bowl and compost the herb material.

Add the remaining ingredients to the tea and stir gently with a spoon or spatula. Slowly pour into a squeezable or pump bottle. To use, pump or squeeze directly onto your scalp and massage your hair, starting at the roots and working down towards the ends. This shampoo will have little lather, but you can add more shampoo for a richer lather if desired. Rinse well and follow with the Held Conditioner below.

HELD CONDITIONER

This conditioner is simple and supportive, just what you need when you're going through a difficult time. It takes all of five minutes to whip up as is, but feel free to infuse the jojoba oil with additional herbal support if you feel called to do so. Thyme and violet are both excellent options.

- 2 oz | 60 ml jojoba oil
- 2 oz | 60 ml aloe vera gel
- 20 drops of tea tree essential oil
- 20 drops of palmarosa essential oil
- 15 drops of basil essential oil
- ½ cup unscented conditioner

Blend together the oil, gel, and essential oils in a small bowl until well combined. Add the conditioner and blend again until smooth. Massage into damp hair and comb through with a wide-toothed comb to detangle. Allow the mixture to stay in your hair for at least 10 minutes and up to 1 hour. Rinse well and style as usual.

HELD BODY WASH

This body wash combines spiritually cleansing powerhouses: peppermint, sweetgrass, apple cider vinegar, and thyme. What I love about these ingredients is that they are each well known for clearing negative energy but they are all very gentle in their approach, especially sweetgrass. Sometimes you need a little tough love when you are going through a rough time, while at other times you just need to feel held and supported. This body wash gives me the feeling of the latter. It's stimulating enough so that I feel refreshed but not so aggressive – energetically speaking – that I feel pressured to move or heal faster than I want to.

- 1 cup boiling water
- 1 cup sweetgrass tea
- 1 cup peppermint-scented Castile soap
- 1 tbs apple cider vinegar
- 1 tsp Thyme Tincture (page 185)

- 20 drops of essential oil

- ½ tsp coconut oil

Make a tea by adding the water to 1 tablespoon of the sweetgrass and allow it to steep for 15 minutes. Strain the liquid from the plant material. Add the remaining ingredients to the sweetgrass tea and stir gently until well mixed. Pour into a pump or squeeze bottle with a tight-fitting lid and use as you would a traditional body wash. The coconut may separate from time to time, so just shake gently to reincorporate it. This mixture can be kept in the refrigerator for three to four weeks, but discard it if you notice a significant change in smell or texture.

SOLAR ECLIPSES

A solar eclipse can only happen during a new moon, when the moon passes between the sun and the earth. This is a period of fresh beginnings and overcoming things from your past that have blocked your success. In the following pages you will find a selection of potions to help you move beyond your past, open yourself up to the future, and regain your personal power.

SOLAR ECLIPSE CORRESPONDENCES

Below is a list of ingredients and symbols that align with the energy of solar eclipses you can use as a starting point for creating your own solar eclipse apothecary potions. Each ingredient has its own properties, bringing something unique to your magical potions. Be sure to check out correspondence tables in Appendix I to discover the individual characteristics of each ingredient.

ESSENTIAL OILS	PLANTS	CRYSTALS
Angelica	Black pepper	Garnet
Basil	Clove	Rainbow moonstone
Benzoin	Dragon's blood	Red jasper
Catnip	Juniper	Red Quartz
Clove	Mullein	Topaz
Juniper	Rue	
Mugwort	St. John's wort	
Myrrh	Thyme	
Patchouli		
Pepper		
Pine		
Rosemary		
Vetiver		

Cord-Cutting Ritual

I have used this ritual for years, and you may have even seen me share it here and there. It's one of the few rituals I have not gone back and redone because I always find it works exactly the way I need it to. I work this ritual whenever I need to move on. You'll know when you need it: when you really want to let something go but it keeps creeping into your mind. That's usually a sign that your energy is still connected with a person, place, or situation and you need to eliminate the connection.

- Citrine Crystal Bath Bar with Rosemary and Black Pepper Melt and Pour Hand Soap (page 198)
- yarn or string
- 1 white candle
- Solar Plexus Power Body Scrub (page 196)

Wash your hands and, if you like, your entire body with the bath bar to completely purify your hands.

Prepare your cords by cutting the yarn into 9 in | 25 cm pieces, making sure you have one string for each person or situation you wish to cut. You can make each string a different color for different people or situations if you wish, but this is not necessary. If not, select yarn in colors that aid with release such as red, white, or blue.

When you are ready to begin, place all of the tools in front of you then cast your circle. Gather up the cords and tie a knot at one end to bind them all together. Hold the cords in your hands and say the following incantation out loud:

I now wish to cut all ties with [insert name or names] from my mind, body, heart, and soul. I acknowledge them for the role(s) they have played in my life, but I know I have outgrown their energy and no longer need their lessons. It is with love and gratitude that I cut them away to make space for new, more loving relationships.

Hold the cords with your right hand. One by one, separate each cord and take a few moments to go through all of the negative emotions you feel for this person or situation. Really let yourself feel these emotions completely: you want to bring up any and everything you wish to let go. When you have brought up everything regarding that person, cut the cord from the bunch with scissors. Repeat the process until you have cut away all of the cords.

Burn the cords one by one in the flame of the candle and place them in a heatproof bowl or dish to continue burning. Finally, take the knotted end and burn that as well. While burning the cords, say the following:

I am free from any attachments I have to these cords. I forgive each and every person for any wrongdoings against me, allowing both myself and them to be free from reattaching. I now have space to invite something new into my life, and I call in spirit to fill this empty space with the deepest desires of my heart. So it is.

Take what's left of the burned cords and ashes and bury them somewhere outside where the energy can be returned to the earth. Finish this ritual by scrubbing yourself with the body scrub to eliminate any residual energy that may be trying to reattach itself to the past.

SOLAR PLEXUS POWER BODY SCRUB

The solar plexus chakra is the seat of your personal power, but you may also be carrying blocks to your success in this area. This scrub will encourage the flow of energy related to reclaiming your power, plus it will inspire that all-over glow that comes from feeling and looking your best. It features citrus, which is not only wonderful for opening your solar plexus chakra but is a wonderful non-abrasive exfoliant to eat away dry and flaky skin. Just be sure to avoid sun exposure after using this scrub, as citrus can cause the skin to be sun sensitive.

- 4 drops of bergamot essential oil
- 4 drops of lemon verbena essential oil
- 4 drops of rosemary essential oil
- ¼ cup sunflower oil
- zest of 1 lemon
- 1 tbs ground flax or hemp seed meal
- 1 cup sea salt

Mix the essential oils with the sunflower oil to combine and set aside. Be sure to wash the lemon thoroughly before zesting, even if you are using an organic lemon. Add the lemon zest, flax, and salt to a clean bowl and mix. Add the oil mixture and blend with a fork to get a uniform consistency. Store the scrub in a clean, sealed container. This mixture will keep for one to two weeks in the refrigerator.

To use, massage small amounts of the scrub into your body, working in circular, clockwise motions. Begin at your solar plexus region to activate the chakra, then go to the bottoms of your feet and work up. Rinse well.

Citrine Crystal Bath Bar with Rosemary and Black Pepper Melt and Pour Hand Soap

Hands pick up a lot of energy, which makes sense when you think about it. How many times a day do you touch handles and doorknobs, pick up things in a grocery store, or touch any number of surfaces that hundreds and potentially thousands of other people have also touched throughout the day? This bar is perfect for cleansing any stray energy thanks to vitality-restoring citrine. Rosemary and black pepper are added to banish any negative energy.

- melt and pour hand soap
- mini crockpot, double broiler, or bain marie
- 1 lb | 500 g tumbled citrine chips 0.5–0.6 in | 12–15 mm in size
- silicone soap molds
- ½ oz | 15 ml rosemary essential oil
- 30 drops of black pepper essential oil

Cut the soap base into small, 1 in | 2.5 cm pieces and place them in the crockpot – one that is not used for food – and turn on the lowest heat setting. Stir every so often to prevent burning.

In the meantime, place a handful of the citrine chips into each cavity of the molds, spreading them out to form single, even layers.

Remove the soap base from the heat once it has completely melted. Allow the mixture to cool for about 5 minutes, then add the essential oils and stir well to blend. Use a ladle to slowly spoon the soap mixture into each cavity of the molds. Pouring slowly will prevent the crystals from moving around, which will cause gaps in the layer.

Cover the molds with a towel once each cavity has been filled and allow the soap to harden overnight. Release the soaps from their molds and store in a dry place to harden further, at least overnight. The longer they sit the harder they will be. Use like any other bar of soap, collecting the crystals in your tub or shower before going down the drain. Re-use the crystals in meditations, rituals, or other ritual potions.

CHAPTER 14

SPECIAL MOONS

BLUE MOON

A blue moon is when there is a second full moon within one calendar month. You may be familiar with the phrase "once in a blue moon," which means something that is very rare or isn't available very often. Spiritually, this is your time to believe in the impossible and take a risk on something that feels like too much for you to accomplish. On the following pages you will find a very simple but effective spray potion to help you overcome your fears of success, along with an easy ritual to help you break through analysis paralysis.

BLUE MOON CORRESPONDENCES

Below is a list of ingredients and symbols that align with the energy of blue moons you can use as a starting point for creating your own blue moon apothecary potions. Each ingredient has its own properties, bringing something unique to your magical potions. Be sure to check out correspondence tables in Appendix I to discover the individual characteristics of each ingredient.

ESSENTIAL OILS	PLANTS	CRYSTALS
Basil	Black peppercorn	Blue calcite
Chamomile	Cedar leaf	Clear quartz
Cinnamon	Cinquefoil	Moldavite
Clove	Frankincense resin	Obsidian
Frankincense	Ginger	Selenite
Lemon	Honeysuckle	White or cream moonstone
Nutmeg	Nutmeg	
Pepper	Yarrow	
Rose		
Sandalwood		

Do It Now Ritual

Indecision or feeling overwhelmed is all too common when you are attempting to achieve goals, and even though you know what you want to do you may find you have no idea where to start. This ritual is simple, but it is intended to take the guesswork out of getting the ball rolling. It works in a similar way to pulling oracle cards, drawing the action that is most needed in a particular moment to you.

- pen
- slips of paper
- Unlimited Spray (see page 204)
- box or bag

Find a quiet place to do this ritual. Bring to mind the goal you would like to accomplish and hold the vision in your mind for several moments, focusing on actions you can take immediately to start working towards this goal.

When you have a clear vision, open your eyes and write down each different action on the paper, one action per slip of paper. Lightly mist the papers with a small amount of the spray; you don't want the papers to be damp.

Put all of the papers into the box and shake it for a few moments to mix up the contents. Close your eyes and take deep breaths until you feel calm and relaxed. Ask yourself what action you need to take most to fulfill your goal of . . . . (fill in the blank).

With your eyes still closed, reach inside the box and pull out one single slip of paper. Open your eyes and read it out loud, which is the most important action to take at this time. Work this step, then repeat the ritual until you have gone through all of the slips of paper.

Unlimited Spray

This is an unusual pairing, as sandalwood doesn't really go with spearmint or eucalyptus traditionally. Somehow, it works here. I made this spray when I was going through a rough time, which is the case for a lot of these blends, and for this one especially I needed a kick of motivation. This mist is all about believing in yourself.

- 14 drops of blue mallee eucalyptus essential oil
- 12 drops of sandalwood essential oil
- 3 drops of spearmint essential oil
- ½ oz | 15 ml witch hazel or ½ oz | 15 ml vodka
- 1.5 oz | 45 ml distilled water
- black obsidian chips, optional

Combine the essential oils with the witch hazel or vodka in a small bowl and mix well. Pour into a 2 oz | 60 ml spray bottle then top off with the water. Add the desired amount of obsidian chips, cap the bottle and shake well. Place the bottle on your altar to synergize for at least 24 hours. Shake well before use to distribute the magic, then mist several times to fill your space with fragrance.

SUPER MOON

The super moon is a new or full moon that occurs when the moon has reached its closest point to the earth. The technical term for this is a "perigee," and the moon looks to be about 14 to 15 percent bigger when this occurs during a full moon. This means the moon's effects have a significantly bigger impact on us during that time: Bigger success, but also bigger emotions. In this section I have provided the recipes for one of my most popular sets of products ever, the Manifestation Spray and Manifestation Oil.

Along with these potions you will find a simple box spell to protect your manifestations from energetic harm, because emotions can run high at this time and you never know when you might piss off someone and they put a curse on you. Just kidding, but you never know . . .

SUPER MOON CORRESPONDENCES

Below is a list of ingredients and symbols that align with the energy of super moons you can use as a starting point for creating your own super moon apothecary potions. Each ingredient has its own properties, bringing something unique to your magical potions. Be sure to check out correspondence tables in Appendix I to discover the individual characteristics of each ingredient.

ESSENTIAL OILS	PLANTS	CRYSTALS
Bergamot	Aloe	Citrine
Grapefruit	Basil	Clear quartz
Jasmine	Bee pollen	Moldavite
Juniper	Frankincense	Selenite
Lemon	Honey	Sunstone
Lime	Motherwort	White or cream moonstone
Mandarin	Orris root	
Myrrh	Peony	
Orange	Pine needles	
Patchouli	Sandalwood	
Sandalwood	Strawberry	
Ylang ylang		

Manifestation Essential Oil Master Blend

This fragrance and the products I used it for are the top-selling products of all time for my brand Spirit Element. Spirit Element evolved quite a bit in 2022, so I don't sell any of the old products anymore although I still get requests to either bring this back or offer the recipe. The super moon is all about super results, so I thought: what better place to offer up this longtime fan favorite? Now you can take advantage of this essential oil blend, which has helped thousands worldwide to manifest their greatest desires.

- 18 drops of jasmine essential oil
- 9 drops of mandarin essential oil
- 3 drops of copaiba balsam essential oil

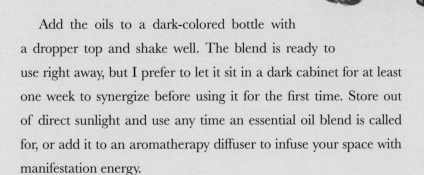

Add the oils to a dark-colored bottle with a dropper top and shake well. The blend is ready to use right away, but I prefer to let it sit in a dark cabinet for at least one week to synergize before using it for the first time. Store out of direct sunlight and use any time an essential oil blend is called for, or add it to an aromatherapy diffuser to infuse your space with manifestation energy.

MANIFESTATION SPRAY

Pretty much every potion I have ever made was born out of my need to deepen my spiritual practice, and this one is no exception. I made this manifestation spray many moons ago as a way to reinforce my new moon intentions. A spritz or two every morning along with a quick prayer goes a long way toward bringing your goals to life.

- 50 drops of Manifestation Essential Oil Master Blend (see page 207)
- ½ oz | 15 ml witch hazel or ½ oz | 15 ml vodka, optional (or use 2 oz | 60 ml water instead if you wish to omit the alcohol)
- 1½ oz | 45 ml distilled water
- handful of citrine chips
- handful of sunstone chips

Combine the master blend with the witch hazel or vodka in a small bowl and mix well. Pour into a 2 oz | 60 ml spray bottle then top off with the water. Add the desired amount of citrine and sunstone chips, cap, and shake well. Place the bottle on your altar to synergize for at least 24 hours. Shake well before use to distribute the magic, then mist several times each day to fill your space and reinforce your intentions.

MANIFESTATION OIL

This oil along with my Manifestation Spray were one of my first ritual sets offered through Spirit Element, and they continued to be a bestseller for a very long time. I like to dab a little bit of this oil onto my vision board and other photos of things that represent my intentions, or on bills of money when I am trying to manifest more wealth.

- 1 tsp gold-colored mica
- 50 drops of Manifestation Essential Oil Master Blend (page 207)
- 1 vitamin E capsule
- 2 tbs almond oil
- 1 tbs olive oil
- 1 tbs grapeseed oil

Mix the mica with the master blend until combined, then pour the mixture into a 2 oz | 60 ml bottle. Prick the vitamin E capsule with a needle and squeeze the contents into the bottle, then fill the bottle with the remaining oils. Cap and shake well. Place the bottle on your altar to synergize for at least 24 hours, then use it as you would a traditional bath and body oil or to adorn ritual tools and candles. The mica will settle to the bottom after a while but will reincorporate easily after a few shakes.

MANIFESTATION PROTECTION BOX

It can take many months or even years for some of your biggest goals to manifest, and in that time many, many things can happen to jeopardize your results. For the really big goals, I make a protection box to shield them from anyone's negative energy, including my own.

- Manifestation Spray (see page 208)
- box with a lid
- smoky quartz
- clear quartz
- black tourmaline
- Manifestation Oil (see page 209)
- 1 tsp black pepper

- black string

- tealight

- wax seal kit with black wax nuggets

Write down on paper your goal in as full detail as you can, then lightly spritz the paper with the Manifestation Spray and place it inside the box. Hold the crystals in your hand, put a few drops of the Manifestation Oil on top and massage it into the crystals.

Place the crystals in the box on top of the paper, then sprinkle over the pepper. Sit quietly with the box in hand and ask your spirit guides, ancestors, deities, god, or whatever cosmic force you believe has your best interest at heart to watch over your goal, keeping  it safe from influences that wish to bring you harm. Thank them once you are done, then close the box firmly and wrap a length of the string around it several times and tie at the top.

Light the tealight. Follow the instructions of the wax kit to melt the wax, then pour it on top of the string where you've tied it. Stick the seal stamp on top and allow it to cool completely before removing. Store the box in a safe place and do not open it until your goal has manifested.

CHAPTER 15

BASIC RECIPES

BASIC BODY SCRUB

- 1 cup fine pink salt or sugar
- 1–2 tsp powdered herbs or spices
- ¼ cup carrier oil
- ½ tsp vitamin E essential oil
- 30 drops of essential oil

In a bowl, whisk together the salt or sugar with the herbs or spices. Using a spoon, combine the dry mixture with the oil. Stir well to blend, then add the essential oils one drop at a time. Stop and blend well every 5 to 10 drops. Spoon into a container with a tight-fitting lid. To apply, massage a small amount onto moist skin, rubbing in a counterclockwise motion, then rinse it off. Use within six to eight months. Refrigeration is not required. The yield is slightly more than one cup.

BASIC BATH SALTS

- 1 cup salt
- ½ cup Epsom Salts
- ½ cup baking soda
- ¼ cup powder or clay (can be a mixture of materials)
- 20 drops of essential oil

Mix together the dry ingredients in a bowl, then add the essential oil and stir well. Spoon into a container or jar with a tight-fighting lid. To use, add the desired amount to a bath and soak for 20 to 30 minutes. Use the remaining mixture within 12 months. The yield is 16 oz | 475 g.

EASY CREAM OR LOTION

- 16 oz | 480 ml unscented lotion or cream
- 50 drops of essential oil

In a medium bowl, blend the lotion and essential oil together. Using a funnel, gently spoon the lotion into a squeeze bottle or one with pump top, allowing it time to settle before adding another spoonful. Use as desired within 12 months. The yield is 16 oz | 480 ml.

Basic Face Mask

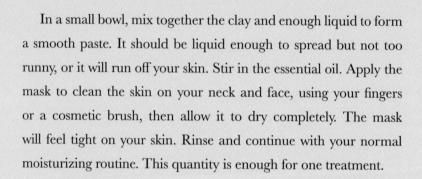

- 1 tbs clay
- 1–2 drops of essential oil

In a small bowl, mix together the clay and enough liquid to form a smooth paste. It should be liquid enough to spread but not too runny, or it will run off your skin. Stir in the essential oil. Apply the mask to clean the skin on your neck and face, using your fingers or a cosmetic brush, then allow it to dry completely. The mask will feel tight on your skin. Rinse and continue with your normal moisturizing routine. This quantity is enough for one treatment.

Basic Spray

- 30–50 drops of essential oil
- 2 cups distilled water, hydrosol, or a combination
- 1 tsp high-proof or infused alcohol, optional

Drop the essential oil into a suitable bottle one drop at a time. Add the liquids and screw on a spray top. Allow the formula to synergize for at least one day, and shake well before each use. Spray as desired. Keep the spray out direct sunlight or choose a dark-colored glass bottle. The spray will stay fresh for up to 12 months if the alcohol is used. The yield is 2 cups.

BASIC BODY WASH

- ½ cup distilled water

- ½ cup hydrosol

- 1 cup Castile soap

- 20 drops of essential oil

- ½ tsp carrier oil

Bring the water to the boil in a small saucepan, then turn off heat. Add the hydrosol, cover, and allow the mixture to steep and cool for at least 30 to 45 minutes. Add your desired herb material, cover and allow the mixture to steep and cool for at least 30 to 45 minutes. Strain and compost the herbs. Add the soap and essential oils to the herbal base and mix well. Pour into a bottle with a tight-fighting lid. This mixture can be kept in the refrigerator for three to four weeks. The yield is 2 cups.

Basic Alcohol Tincture

- plant material of choice
- high-proof alcohol
- waxed paper
- cheesecloth or coffee filters

Fill a jar with the plant material, leaving about 1 in | 2.5 cm of room at the top. Cover the plant material with the alcohol, still leaving some space at the top. Put the waxed paper over the mouth of the jar and screw on a tight-fitting lid. Shake the jar to distribute evenly, adding more alcohol if needed to cover the plant material.

Label the jar with the name and date and put it in a dark place. Shake the jar every day for two to four weeks. The longer it sits the more potent it will be. Strain the plant material through the cheesecloth, pressing out as much of the oil as possible. Compost the plant material. Pour the tincture into an amber-colored dropper bottle and label. Add ½ to 1 teaspoon of tincture to water-based formulas as desired. The yield is 1 cup.

Basic Oil Infusion

A basic oil infusion is one of the best ways to customize creams, balms, and any other apothecary recipe requiring a vegetable oil. The combinations are endless. Use this method to make a botanical body oil or use the infused oil to make a botanical salve.

- dried herbs
- carrier oil or blend of oils
- cheesecloth
- jar with tight lid

MACERATION METHOD

Add the desired herbs to a jar, filling it to three-quarters of the way. Pour in enough oil to fill up the jar completely, and cover the jar with a piece of cheesecloth and cap with a tight-fitting lid. Keep the jar in a sunny or warm space for two to four weeks and shake the mixture daily, especially if you are using cheesecloth. Strain the mixture through the cheesecloth and compost the plant material.

Store the mixture in a jar or bottle with a tight lid for up to one year. Throw away immediately if the oil smells rancid or develops any sign of bacterial growth.

CROCKPOT METHOD

Add the desired herbs to a small crockpot or double broiler and pour over enough oil to cover the plant material completely. Cook on low for 2 to 3 hours, then remove from the heat and allow to cool. Strain and store the mixture following the directions in the maceration method.

Basic Salve Recipe

Below is my basic, go-to salve recipe that I customize based on my needs: this is a must have in any apothecary cabinet. I use these salve variations for everything from dry skin to healing wounds and scars. You can customize the carrier oil by infusing it with a variety of plant materials.

- 1 oz | 30 g beeswax
- 4 oz | 120 ml infused carrier oil (or mixture of oils)
- 1 tbs shea butter
- 20 drops of essential oil

Add all of the ingredients to a double boiler, stirring regularly to prevent burning. Once melted, remove from the heat and allow the mixture to cool slightly, then add the desired essential oil.

Pour or ladle the mixture into a heat-safe container or tin while it is still liquid. Allow the mixture to cool and harden, then cap with a tight-fitting lid. Store in a cool space for up to one year. This salve can be kept in the refrigerator on hot days to prevent melting. To use, scoop a bit with your fingers, gently warm between your palms, and apply as needed.

APPENDIX I

CORRESPONDENCE TABLES

In this appendix you will find a list of ingredients and their properties as they relate to the moon. Many of these ingredients have far more properties than what is listed here, and there are dozens more ingredients that aren't on this list. These are simply the ingredients I enjoy using most in my moon work and how I choose to use them. As always, feel free to take what you need and leave the rest. If you feel called to work with an ingredient in a way other than what is listed here, follow that instinct and see where it leads as it's likely your higher self guiding you to an expression of this ingredient that is uniquely your own.

Likewise, if you feel called to explore ingredients that are not on the list, consider following that ping as well. Discovering your own correspondences with an ingredient makes the process and the result truly your own. This is especially true for ingredients that are native to specific countries that others may not have access to or even know about.

CORRESPONDENCE TABLE:

ESSENTIAL OILS

INGREDIENT	MOON PHASE	PROPERTIES
Bergamot	New, first quarter, last quarter, super	Manifestation, success, wealth, dealing with problems, confidence
Cinnamon	New, first quarter, blue	High vibrations, luck, money, balance, success, spirituality
Chamomile	New, full, blue	Healing, peace, creativity, manifestation, success

INGREDIENT	MOON PHASE	PROPERTIES
Lemon	New, first quarter, full, super	Clarity, success, raising vibrations, happiness, purification, spiritual connection
Myrrh	New, super, solar eclipse	Overcoming negativity and spiritual blocks, transformation, balance, strength
Neroli	New, full	Beauty, confidence, awareness, peace, creativity
Oakmoss	New, waxing, waning	Grounding, abundance, manifestation, finding purpose
Opoponax	New	Purity, growth, renewal, transformation
Orange	New, last quarter, super	Creativity, awareness, happiness, confidence, self-care, strength
Patchouli	New, last quarter, super, lunar eclipse, solar eclipse	Growth, grounding, abundance, restoring peace, overcoming negativity and problems
Sandalwood	New, full, last quarter, blue, super	Restoring peace, renewal, overcoming the past, meditation, emotional healing, creativity
Angelica	Full, waxing, solar eclipse	Banishing, balance, renewal, purity, beauty
Anise	Waxing	Stimulating, growth, change, well-being
Benzoin	Waxing, last quarter, solar eclipse	Success, abundance, inspiration, healing, wisdom
Clary sage	Waxing, full, lunar eclipse	Finding purpose, clear mind, intuition, peace, clarity, prosperity, making changes

INGREDIENT	MOON PHASE	PROPERTIES
Geranium	Waxing	Growth, self-awareness, success, courage, attraction
Juniper	Waxing, waning gibbous, last quarter, super, solar eclipse	Purity, banishing, psychic abilities, grounding, abundance, growth, transformation
Lemon balm	Waxing, full, last quarter	Peace, emotional healing, finding purpose, clarity, well-being, success
Mugwort	Waxing	Awareness, growth, happiness, psychic abilities
Palma rosa	Waxing	Growth, life purpose, courage, taking action
Peppermint	Waxing, first quarter, lunar eclipse	Prosperity, clarity, overcoming negativity, self-worth, well-being
Tea tree	Waxing, last quarter, lunar eclipse	Confidence, purity, growth, emotional and physical healing
Thyme	Waxing, full, waning gibbous, last quarter	Clearing, purifying, well-being, renewal, growth, strength, courage
Allspice	First quarter	Prosperity, determination, raising energy, attraction
Basil	First quarter, blue, solar eclipse	Taking action, courage, confidence, success, growth, manifestation
Cardamom	First quarter	Creativity, confidence, courage
Clove	First quarter, last quarter, blue, solar eclipse	Success, attraction (especially money), personal growth, creativity, purity, banishing
Ginger	First quarter, last quarter	Emotional healing, well-being, prosperity

INGREDIENT	MOON PHASE	PROPERTIES
Lime	First quarter, super	Prosperity, self-care, energy, confidence
Petitgrain	First quarter, last quarter	Growth, awareness, confidence, inner reflection
Pine	First quarter, waning gibbous, solar eclipse	Peace, balance, transformation, confidence, renewal, banishing, prosperity
Pepper	First quarter, blue, solar eclipse	Overcoming problems, courage, success, prosperity, strength
Rosemary	First quarter, full, last quarter, waning gibbous, solar eclipse	Grief, clearing, recovery, healing, banishing, clarity
Sage	First quarter, waning gibbous, last quarter, blue, lunar eclipse	Clearing, peace, grounding, prosperity, wisdom, well-being
Vetiver	First quarter, solar eclipse	Grounding, prosperity, overcoming sorrow, longevity
Ylang ylang/canaga	Full, super, lunar eclipse	Peace, inner reflection, transitions
Hyssop	Full, waning gibbous, lunar eclipse	Attraction, clarity, purity
Jasmine	All phases	Beauty, confidence, intuition, manifestation, clear communication, healing, perhaps the most "moon" oil of all
Frankincense	Full, last quarter, blue	Meditation, clarity, courage, renewal, transformation, clearing
Marjoram	Full, waning gibbous, last quarter	Healing, releasing, protection, growth, self-care, grief
Rose	Full, blue	Love, wisdom, blessings, strength, self-love, courage, sorrow

INGREDIENT	MOON PHASE	PROPERTIES
Cedarwood	Full, last quarter	Grounding, growth, renewal, well-being, abundance, purity, confidence, success
Lavender	Full, last quarter	All purpose oil, peace, clarity, purity, strength, well-being
Valerian	Waning gibbous	Overcoming problems, love, grounding, well-being, peace
Amyris	Waning gibbous	Transformation, spiritual connection, cycles, balance, purpose
Eucalyptus	Waning gibbous, blue	Healing, overcoming negativity, banishing, strength
Fennel	Waning gibbous, lunar eclipse	Protection, transformation, balance, healing, renewal
Fir needle	Waning gibbous, last quarter, lunar eclipse	Growth, expression, cycles, renewal, strength, restoring hope
Spearmint	Last quarter, blue	Purity, truth, awareness, healing, growth
Cypress	Last quarter, lunar eclipse	Grounding, banishing, focus, strength, wisdom, transformation, inner reflection
Spruce hemlock	Last quarter, lunar eclipse	Intuition, restoring hope, renewal, overcoming problems, inspiration, clarity
Caraway	Last quarter, lunar eclipse	Cycles, confidence, renewal
Nutmeg	Last quarter, blue	Clarity, prosperity, change, cycles, releasing
Mandarin	Super	Abundance, success, manifestation, happiness

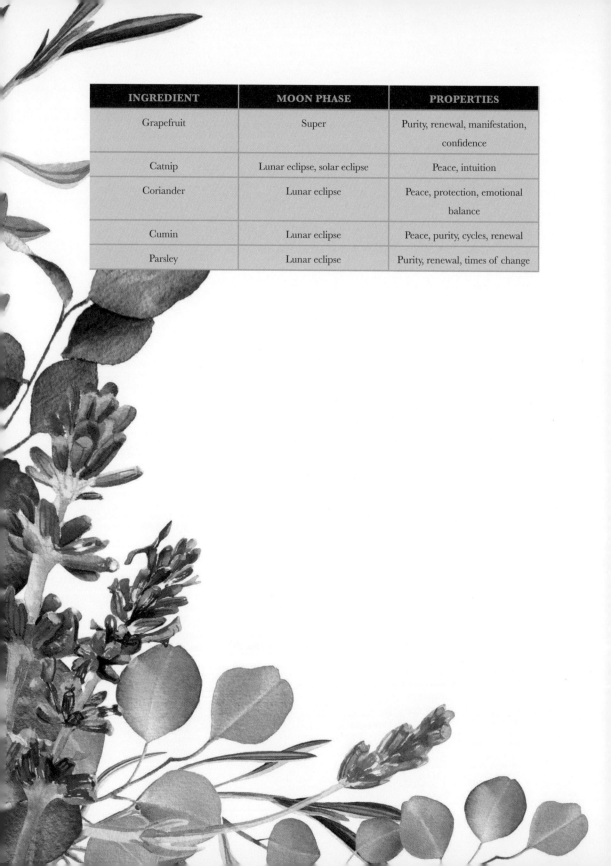

INGREDIENT	MOON PHASE	PROPERTIES
Grapefruit	Super	Purity, renewal, manifestation, confidence
Catnip	Lunar eclipse, solar eclipse	Peace, intuition
Coriander	Lunar eclipse	Peace, protection, emotional balance
Cumin	Lunar eclipse	Peace, purity, cycles, renewal
Parsley	Lunar eclipse	Purity, renewal, times of change

CORRESPONDENCE
TABLE:

PLANTS

INGREDIENT	MOON PHASE	PROPERTIES
Frankincense resin	New, blue, super	Manifestation, success, clearing, meditation
Bamboo	New	Protection, good luck
Chamomile	New	Meditation, increase, peace, good luck
Cinnamon	New	Success, protection, power, prosperity, raising energy

INGREDIENT	MOON PHASE	PROPERTIES
Clove	New, solar eclipse	Protection, prosperity
Honeysuckle	New, first quarter, blue	Prosperity, success, attraction, confidence
Tonka bean	New	Prosperity, courage, success, taking action
Balsam fir	New, first quarter	Progress, change, clarity
Milk thistle	Waxing	Wisdom, strength
Oak	Waxing	Wisdom, strength
Peach	Waxing	Love, well-being, wisdom
Sage	Waxing, last quarter, lunar eclipse	Wisdom, purity, well-being, healing, clarity
Sunflower	Waxing	Power, energy
Five finger grass	All phases	All-purpose herb
Elderberry/ flower	Waxing	Protection
Ginger	First quarter, blue	Prosperity, success, well-being, energy
High John	First quarter	Confidence, success, prosperity, protection
Motherwort	First quarter, super	Confidence, success
Yarrow	First quarter, blue	Courage, confidence, healing, love, intuition
Cedar leaf	First quarter, full, blue	Strength, grounding, prosperity, confidence
Allspice	First quarter	Healing, prosperity
Vervain	First quarter	Prosperity, creativity, peace, healing
Jasmine	Full	Intuition, prosperity, love, beauty, creativity

INGREDIENT	MOON PHASE	PROPERTIES
Peppermint	Full, waxing gibbous, waning gibbous, lunar eclipse	Healing, peace, purity, prosperity
Lemon	Full	Raising energy, cleansing, purifying
Orange	Full, last quarter	Prosperity, happiness, love, attraction
Aloe vera	Full, super	Protection, peace, new love
White willow bark	Full	Healing, overcoming negativity
Angelica root	Full, last quarter	Protection, purity, patience, releasing
Moss	Waning gibbous	Strength, protection
Orris root	Waning gibbous, super	Communication, success
Poppy seed	Waning gibbous	Awareness
Saffron	Waning gibbous	Love, restoring happiness, healing, strength
Star anise	Waning gibbous	Awareness
Pine needles	Last quarter, super	Prosperity, grounding, success, purification
Patchouli	Last quarter	Prosperity, grounding, awareness
Coffee	Waxing gibbous, last quarter	Grounding, peace
Barley	Last quarter	Protection, healing
Tarragon	Last quarter	Emotional healing
Sea salt	Last quarter	Purifying, grounding, clearing, banishing, protection
Calendula	Last quarter	Raising energy, protection, intuition
Olive leaf	Waxing gibbous, last quarter	Healing, peace
Horehound	Last quarter	Protection, clarity, creativity

INGREDIENT	MOON PHASE	PROPERTIES
Carnation	Waxing gibbous, last quarter	Strength, balance
Lily	Last quarter	Renewal
Lavender	Waxing gibbous, last quarter	Peace, purity, harmony
Thyme	Last quarter, lunar eclipse, solar eclipse	Grief, clearing, healing, courage, peace
Eucalyptus	Blue	Healing, protection, purity
Nutmeg	Blue	Prosperity, protection
Black pepper	Blue, solar eclipse	Banishing, protection
Honey/bee pollen	Super	Love, attraction, happiness
Strawberry	Super	Success
Peony	Super	Prosperity, success
Basil	First quarter, blue, super	Protection, prosperity, success
Sandalwood	Super	Healing, meditation, manifestation
Witch hazel	Lunar eclipse	Grief, protection
Violet	Lunar eclipse	Creativity, peace
Marjoram	Lunar eclipse	Cleansing, grief
Mullein	Solar eclipse	Protection, courage, banishing
St. John's Wort	Solar eclipse	Banishing, protection, restoring light
Rue	Solar eclipse	Healing, protection, banishing
Juniper leaf/berry	Solar eclipse	Health, prosperity, love
Dragon's blood resin	Solar eclipse	Protection, banishing, overcoming poor habits, success

CRYSTALS

INGREDIENT	MOON PHASE	PROPERTIES
Citrine	New, waxing	Manifestation, wealth, success
Clear quartz	New, full	Manifestation, intention setting, clearing, raising vibrations, clarity
Black moonstone	New	Success, inspiration, shadow work
Labradorite	New	Manifestation, intuition, protection, expression

INGREDIENT	MOON PHASE	PROPERTIES
Himalayan salt	All phases	Love (especially self-love), gentle grounding, protection
Moonstone	All phases	Protection, love, support, acceptance, healing
Selenite	Full	Clearing, light, awareness, meditation
Moldavite	Waxing, full	Inner reflection, awakening, transformation
Angelite	Waxing gibbous, full, waning	Nurturing, awareness, peace, cleansing
Amethyst	All phases	Creativity, intuition, healing, protection, surrender, meditation
Lepidolite	Waning	Peace, clearing blocks, dealing with transitions
Sodalite	Last quarter, new	Wisdom, intuition, truth, inspiration
Howlite	Waxing gibbous, last quarter	Patience, calming, contemplation, self-care

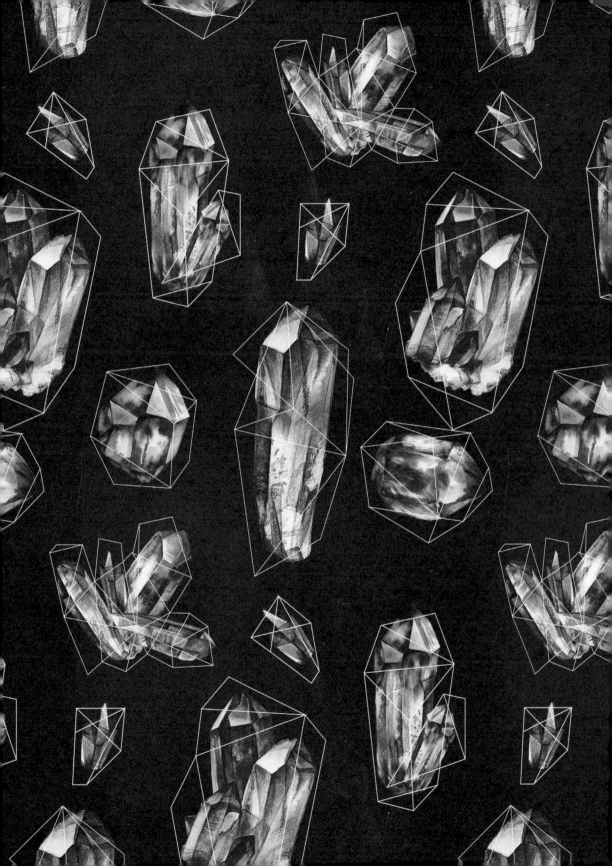

APPENDIX II

THE MOON SIGNS OF THE ZODIAC

MOON ENERGY IN ASTROLOGY

This book is about creating moon-inspired beauty and ritual potions but, being a celestial body, I would be remiss if I didn't mention at least some of the moon's astrological influence. You do not need to be familiar with astrology or know the placement of your moon sign to work with the moon phases, but it does provide an extra layer of awareness that you can leverage when making your next lunar blend.

The moon in astrology represents the inner landscape, or what I call being *inner SELF-Centered*. Moon signs teach you about your internal cycles, such as changes in your mood or energy levels. It is the fastest-moving celestial body of the zodiac, and the only planet that has more influence is the sun.

I would even argue the moon's influence is much more critical. The sun represents your core personality and ultimate purpose in life, but the moon represents how you see yourself and also how you manage your day-to-day emotions. Your self-image can either support or suppress your natural personality. If you're a powerful public speaker but have low self-esteem, you may find it challenging to speak in front of a crowd despite having a naturally commanding voice and presence. So while the sun will tell you who you're meant to be, the moon is responsible for developing your self-worth, helping you achieve your mission. And if you don't have self-worth, you'll find it much more difficult to step into your destiny.

This is why Cancer comes before Leo in the astrological progression. Leo is ruled by the sun and is the sign of shining your light, but knowing your purpose and not being confident enough to share that with the world is almost the same as not having a purpose at all. The universe gives you the moon's energy first so you can begin to trust yourself, your intuition, and develop self-confidence. Once you make it to the sun, you'll be prepared to tackle your biggest dreams.

DO YOU HAVE STRONG MOON ENERGY?

Knowing your moon sign is ideal, but you can still identify strong or weak moon manifestations without it. Someone with strong moon energy will have many of the following:

- Emotional intelligence.
- The ability to readily accept support from others including compliments, help, and constructive criticism.
- Makes self-development a priority and regularly spends time in self-reflection.
- A strong sense of self and is not easily influenced by external forces.
- A strong ability to discern truth from fiction and trusts in "gut feelings."
- A good listener: You are watchful of your environment, taking in not just verbal communication but body language as well. You're also great at reading a room.
- You are in touch with your body: You are aware of changes in your mood and energy and funnel that awareness into a rich practice of self-care.

Someone with a weak manifestation of moon energy will be more like the following:

- Emotionally suppressed: You may find it difficult to share your emotions with others or to allow yourself to feel emotions.

- Lack of emotional connection with others.

- Intense mood swings and very little to no inner peace.

- Highly introverted, timid, shy, and fearful.

- Emotionally reactive and unable to receive help or criticism.

- A tendency to play the victim or project your feelings onto others.

- Highly aggressive and forceful.

- Self-absorbed and unable to make space for others.

- Gullible.

- Low self-esteem and self-worth as well as an inability to take action.

THE MOON IN THE 12 ZODIAC SIGNS

The moon has eight cycles, and each of these cycles transits through the 12 zodiac signs throughout the year. Knowing which sign the moon is in when making your moon potions can add an extra layer of influence to your recipes, and it can also help you have a better understanding of how the moon affects you personally. It isn't at all necessary to consider astrology when making moon potions, but if you are interested it's a good idea to become familiar with your personal moon sign and have an understanding of how the moon behaves in each of the 12 signs.

Locate your moon sign on your birth chart, then find your moon sign below and explore some of the positive and negative expressions of this sign. This will be your starting place for learning to use your moon energy for your benefit rather than letting it get the better of you. If you don't have a birth chart you can obtain help in preparing one by searching "create my birth chart" online. You will need your location and date and time of birth.

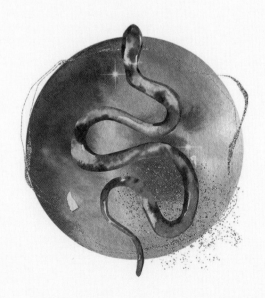

MOON IN ARIES

This placement is easily able to articulate desires, needs, and dreams. However, they see emotional displays as weak and are turned off by emotions in others. They can be emotionally selfish and find it challenging to compromise. Vulnerability does not come easy for this placement.

Because the moon represents desires and Aries represents actions, this placement is great at knowing and acting upon dreams. Your instincts are well developed and you trust yourself completely, which comes in handy for all your innovative ideas. You turn ideas into reality with ease.

With this placement you must learn to open yourself emotionally. You love the chase of a relationship, but can get bored once you've reached your goal. Finding new hobbies and activities or starting fresh projects are great ways to keep this placement in balance.

MOON IN TAURUS

This placement is stubborn and you don't really like to change your opinion. You have a strong sense of your emotions but you aren't one to have mood swings. When you feel a shift in your emotional state, you take the time to sit with your feelings. This can cause you to stay stagnant in one feeling for much longer than is healthy.

You may find yourself spending days, weeks, or longer working through one emotion at a time.

The plus side to your stubborn ways is that you are very stable in your emotions. It isn't often that you get your feathers ruffled and you can keep your cool, especially while in public. Swift change throws you off your game, however, and causes emotional distress. Your emotional state is most balanced when you are in predictable situations.

The home is very important to this placement. Taurus energy values luxury and the moon rules the home. You would do well to spend time making your home as comfortable, luxe, and grounded as possible. You may also enjoy activities such as gardening, knitting, or any activity with defined steps that can be easily repeated.

MOON IN GEMINI

Gemini moons value intellect over emotions, but can also be effective emotional communicators. You find it easy to understand not just your own emotions, but others as well. You have a strong sense of what motivates people and you enjoy analyzing other people's moods. You can "read the room," perhaps better than any other sign.

Your downfall comes in wanting to analyze emotions rather than feel them. You will dissect every part of your emotional landscape, almost as though you're observing from a distance. You must remember to feel your emotions instead of trying to create a step-by-step plan to just "get over" them. Additionally, you may think you're great at getting over emotions rapidly, but this is to a fault. You could do with additional time between mood swings.

Stimulating conversations build your self-worth. You like situations where you can express your intelligence. It's essential to have a partner or social circle of people who can banter with you and engage your strong word sense. Writing, debate, and public speaking are excellent activities for keeping this energy balanced.

MOON IN CANCER

Cancer is the moon's home sign and where its energy is most comfortable. The moon and Cancer both rule the home and family, which are extremely important to people with this placement. The home must feel safe, warm, and comfortable for you to maintain balance and emotional stability.

However, you are prone to moodiness, even in the most comfortable of homes. Your psychic senses are generally on overdrive and you can pick up on emotions in others, sometimes before they know themselves. The problem with this is that you have a hard time distinguishing your emotions from those around you. You must learn to discern your personal feelings, otherwise you might become emotionally overwhelmed and retreat further into yourself.

The moon rules the stomach, the vessel that receives nourishment. Cooking, gardening, and acts of self-care are wonderful activities for bringing the energy of this placement into balance. When it comes to relationships, you need someone who is emotionally stable. This person will allow you the time and space you need to understand your own emotions without external influence. Because you're a homebody, having a partner who enjoys home life is also ideal.

MOON IN LEO

You direct a flair for performance to those closest to you when you have the moon in Leo. Leo is the creative and the performer and needs an audience to feel balanced. You enjoy entertaining and the praise that comes with throwing elaborate dinner parties or cooking a five-course meal on a Wednesday night, but you can become moody and manipulative if your efforts are not well received. You enjoy spoiling those around you, but you must learn to do it for your own validation rather than seeking praise from others.

This placement can be quite playful, and you have more than enough energy to go around. Seek partners who also have high amounts of energy and willingly embrace spontaneous playful moods. Another thing to be mindful of is your ego: you enjoy praise but can quickly spiral into self-centeredness and arrogance. Focus on creative endeavors to bring your energy back into balance.

MOON IN VIRGO

Virgo is the self-development sign and the moon rules self-worth. When these two come together, you are eager to be emotionally healthy but might become too critical in your attempt to do so. Self-criticism is a challenge with this placement. Be mindful of putting yourself down for being less than perfect – there is no such thing as a perfect emotion.

You have a generous heart and are most at balance when you're helping others, but be wary about forgetting your own needs in favor of others. You become moody when your needs are not being met but also when you aren't giving to others. You need a healthy sense of both. Alternating between self-care and acts of service such as volunteering or picking up a chore for your partner is the key to maintaining emotional balance.

MOON IN LIBRA

The keyword for this placement is beauty. As a Libra moon, aesthetically pleasing design is critical for your emotional well-being. This is especially true in the home and in your personal hobbies. Engaging in home decor, art, poetry, or even performance art helps you to stay balanced.

You are the most loyal friend and partner, but you can lose yourself in others in an effort to avoid confrontation. You must learn to develop a stronger sense of self, otherwise people will see you as manipulative and inauthentic. Where you really shine is by your generous heart: you are no stranger to big romantic gestures, and will roll out the red carpet for people who are lucky enough to have you as a friend or partner.

Your superpower is your ability to help others heal emotionally. You have a strong sense of how to maintain balance even though you don't always apply your natural wisdom to yourself. You may struggle with knowing your personal desires, and must remember to spend time discovering your own happiness.

MOON IN SCORPIO

Perhaps the most complex sign for the moon is Scorpio. The moon isn't comfortable here. The moon is passive and gentle while Scorpio is intense and forceful, although Scorpio and the moon can work well together when you tap into their commonality – they both have the ability to flow through cycles of life with ease. Scorpio is the healer, shaman, and transformer. When the moon is in Scorpio, you are likely to be a psychological wiz. You can see through people as though they are glass and you know, almost instantly, what people need to overcome their challenges. Because you see people's motivations and weaknesses with such ease, you run the risk of being manipulative. You don't mean to, of course, so you must learn to recognize this behavior.

Your emotions are best when you confront them head-on. This sign has the greatest potential to heal from emotional instability. The challenge is that your emotions are so intense that you can easily drown in them, so you must learn to confront your fears and then get to know them as friends. Eventually, you will learn to bend your fears to facilitate success. If you do not do this, you can fall into depression or addiction.

MOON IN SAGITTARIUS

You are happiest when you have a sense of freedom. You love to learn and you want to know everything about a subject. You will travel the world if it means you can master something. You have a difficult time sitting still, so it's important to stay busy to keep your emotions in balance. Your restlessness can be challenging for relationships, as you always have a new idea or are eager to go somewhere and you may not settle down until later in life. You will need to learn to ground your energy or find a partner who is equally adventurous.

Sagittarius is the sign of the higher thinker, and if you have this placement you may come across as rude and crass. You make friends easily because you are naturally curious, which translates to taking an interest in others. However, your need for freedom might come across as superficial interest and fleeting. Others might think you are using them or are only interested for a short period of time.

You are an excellent teacher and speak quite eloquently, but you can be so frank that you come across as cold. This couldn't be further from the truth, because you are quite warm and friendly. Learn to think before you speak and consider other people's emotions. Finally, you must learn to form intimate relationships with others. Use your powers of curiosity to stay engaged.

MOON IN CAPRICORN

Capricorn is the moon's weakest placement. The moon is all about emotional expression, which Capricorn avoids almost like the plague. Capricorn does not believe in public displays of affection. You would rather rule by fear than by heart, but despite this you can be quite warm in close relationships. The problem is letting anyone get close enough to know you on this level.

You are ambitious and are going to have to accept that. Your emotional well-being is tied to how successful you are. Your biggest challenge is learning to thrive in business or your career without losing your morals. The more successful you are, the more you will have to work to express your emotions. You must learn to see emotions as valuable rather than something to fear. If you can do this, you will become a compassionate leader who is not only successful in your own right, but you'll also have the ability to inspire greatness in others.

MOON IN AQUARIUS

Aquarius moon's can get over heartbreak with rapid ease. You tend to concentrate your emotions at one time, causing a lightning strike effect that is quick and to the point. You may be explosive, but then you move on and have an unusual ability to forgive.

Rebellion is how you feel emotionally balanced, and your self-worth comes from knowing you are dancing to the beat of your own drum. You must give in to the urge to go against the grain. The worst thing you can do for your emotional well-being is to try to fit in. Pursue activities that allow you to invent things, focus on humanitarian efforts, or make use of technology and innovation.

You can be quite detached from your relationships as well as your emotions. You move through emotions so quickly that it is second nature for you to simply get over things and you expect others to do the same, but most people do not have the capacity to let go with such ease. You must make space for people who need longer periods of time to process their emotions. You may see this as weak, but if you can overcome that you will have the potential to be a great therapist, helping others to deal with their pain in creative and effective ways.

MOON IN PISCES

The moon may feel most at home in Cancer, but this placement is the most emotionally sensitive of all the signs. You are incredibly intuitive: it's as though you can feel the emotions of the entire world all at once. You understand others in a way most never will, and you have compassion for everyone no matter their faults. You can see a path to world peace with ease, and in your heart you know you are meant to facilitate such a utopian world.

Your challenge is getting lost in fantasy. The real world can be a harsh place for this placement, because you hate to see harm coming to others and may choose to live in a fantastical world to avoid such realities. Activities that allow you to tap into your imagination are ideal. Anything having to do with art and fluidity such as photography, writing, dance, pottery, film making and the like are good hobbies or careers for you.

In relationships, look for people with a firm grasp on reality. If you can, find others who will handle everyday tasks while you create. You teach others how to value things other than material possessions, but you must also learn to be more in the present. Balance comes from bringing the beautiful creations of your mind into the physical world.

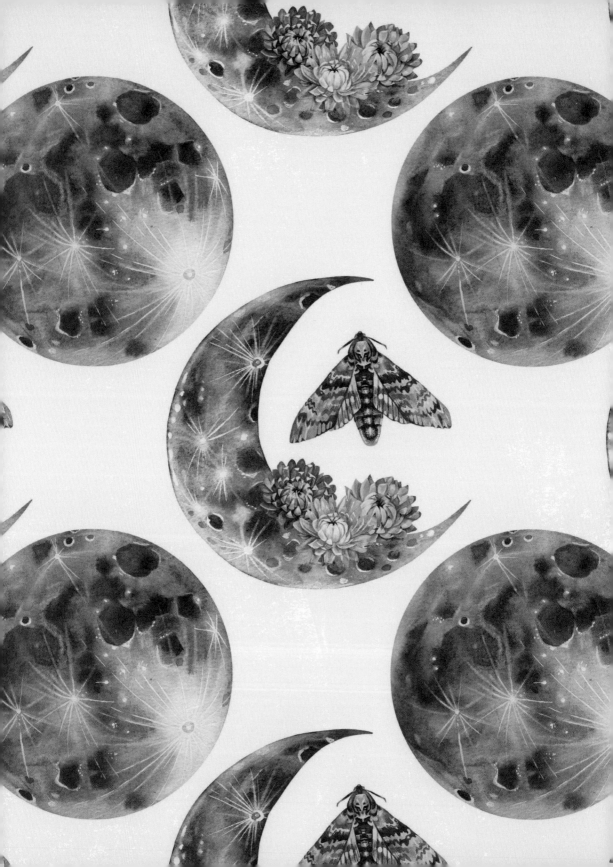

BIBLIOGRAPHY

Alexander, Skye, 2019, *Magickal Astrology: Use the Power of the Planets to Create an Enchanted Life*, Weiser Books, Massachusetts, USA

Binney, Ruth, 2019, *Plant Lore and Legend: The Wisdom and Wonder of Plants and Flowers Revealed*, Dover Publications, West Sussex, UK

Blankenship, Jana, 2019, *Wild Beauty: Wisdom & Recipes for Natural Self-care*, Ten Speed Press, New York, USA

Buhner, Stephen Harrod, 1996, 2001, 2006, *Sacred Plant Medicine: Explorations in the Practice of Indigenous Herbalism*, Bear & Company, Vermont, USA

Chang, T. Susan, 2018, *Tarot Correspondences: Ancient Secrets for Everyday Readers*, Llewellyn Publications, Minnesota, USA

Cunningham, Scott, 1982, 1983, *Magical Herbalism: The Secret Craft of the Wise*, Llewellyn Publications. Minnesota, USA

Cunningham, Scott, 1985, *Cunningham's Encyclopedia of Magical Herbs*, Llewellyn Publications, Minnesota, USA

Harrison, Karen, 2020, *The Herbal Alchemist's Handbook: A Complete Guide to Magickal Herbs and How to Use Them*, Weiser Books, Massachusetts, USA

Illes, Judika, 2005, *Encyclopedia of Witchcraft: The Complete A–Z for the Entire Magical World*, Harper One, New York, USA

Illes, Judika, 2016, *The Big Book of Practical Spells: Everyday Magic That Works*, Weiser Books, Massachusetts, USA

Kipfer, Dr. Barbara Ann, 2014, *Breath Perception: A Daily Guide to Stress Relief, Mindfulness, and Inner Peace*, Helios Press, New York, USA

Kynes, Sandra, 2013, *Llewellyn's Complete Book of Correspondences: A Comprehensive & Cross-Referenced Resource for Pagans & Wiccans*, Llewellyn Publications, Minnesota, USA

Kynes, Sandra, 2013, *Mixing Essential Oils for Magic: Aromatic Alchemy for Personal Blends*, Llewellyn Publications, Minnesota, USA

Kynes, Sandra, 2017, *Plant Magic: A Year of Green Wisdom for Pagans & Wiccans*, Llewellyn Publication, Minnesota, USA

Kynes, Sandra, 2019, *Llewellyn's Complete Book of Essential Oils: How to Blend, Diffuse, Create Remedies, and Use in Everyday Life*, Llewellyn Publications, Minnesota, USA

Moura, Ann, 2003, *Grimoire for the Green Witch: A Book of Shadows*, Llewellyn Publications, Minnesota, USA

Moura, Ann, 2010, *Mansions of the Moon for the Green Witch: A Complete Book of Lunar Magic*, Llewellyn Publications, Minnesota, USA

Murphy-Hiscock, Arin, 2020, *Spellcrafting: Strengthen the Power of Your Craft by Creating and Casting Your Own Unique Spells*, Adams Media, Massachusetts, USA

Popham, Sajah, 2019, *Evolutionary Herbalism: Science, Spirituality, and Medicine from the Heart of Nature*, North Atlantic Books, California, USA

Purchon, Nerys, 2006, The *Natural Health Bible: The Complete Guide to Herbs & Oils, Natural Remedies & Nutrition*, Millennium House Pty Ltd, Sydney, Australia

Shoman, Leah, 2022, *Crystal Rituals by the Moon: Raising Your Vibration Through Every Lunar Cycle*, Rockpool Publishing, Sydney, Australia

Vadhera, Shalini, 2006, *Passport to Beauty: Secrets and Tips From Around the World for Becoming a Global Goddess*, St. Martin's Griffin, New York, USA

Whitehurst, Tess, 2010, *Magical Housekeeping: Simple Charms & Practical Tips for Creating a Harmonious Home*, Llewellyn Publications, Minnesota, USA

Worwood, Valerie Ann, 1991, *The Complete Book of Essential Oils and Aromatherapy*, New World Library, California, USA

ACKNOWLEDGEMENTS

To the years 2022 and 2023 for all of the ways you've removed what no longer served me in my life. For all of the community you have brought me all over the world, and for showing me what I value most. I know I am made stronger because of my challenges.

And for anyone who is reading these words now, I acknowledge the strength in you. I dedicate this book to your blooming magnificence. I know there is so much light you have to give to the world. I may not know your name or your face, but we are connected through spirit and I am cheering for you, always.

ABOUT
THE AUTHOR

Lorriane Anderson is a multidisciplinary spiritual teacher, writer, and soul-based entrepreneur whose work focuses heavily on intentional and energetic living as well as using spiritual practices as a pathway for profound healing, growth, and transformation. She has been featured in *The Daily Star, The Spruce, Reader's Digest, Kindred Spirit*, and *Oprah Daily* among others. She is the author of *The Witch's Apothecary* as well as several other titles in the spiritual space, and is co-creator of the bestselling *Seasons of the Witch* oracle deck series.

SPIRITELEMENT.CO | @SPIRITELEMENT

BONUS
MATERIAL

————— ·····•»)·+)·※·(·(·(·°····· ·····—————

To access exclusive material from the author for readers of *The Moon Apothecary*,
sign up at spiritelement.co/themoonapothecarybonuscontent.

THE WITCH'S APOTHECARY

How to make magical potions for the Wheel of the Year

ISBN: 9781925946796

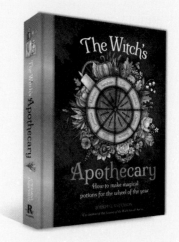

A practical guide for beginning and advanced witches to unlock the greater powers of making your own apothecary blends. Lorriane owns and operates her own successful, soul-based apothecary and uses her own practices to teach you how to make potions based on your needs, intentions, and energy.

A sacred living lifestyle is like slow living, and spiritually infused and focused on mindfulness, magic and self-care. Learn to craft magical blends that carefully follow the Wheel of the Year. You will feel empowered to craft your own formulas for personal use, experiment, and work from nature to create magical blends which tie into sacred sabbat days and tip into your magical energy.

Imagine creating your own candle to improve and appreciate Abundance in your life. Or creating an incense to clear blocks in your life to love.

Learn about the various ingredients, practices, and exercises needed to begin your magical journey and start your own witchy apothecary. You will also find a selection of over 100 recipes associated with each of the sabbats in the Wheel of the Year, and instructions on how to deepen your connection with nature through these seasonal cycles.

Available from all good book stores

rockpoolpublishing.com

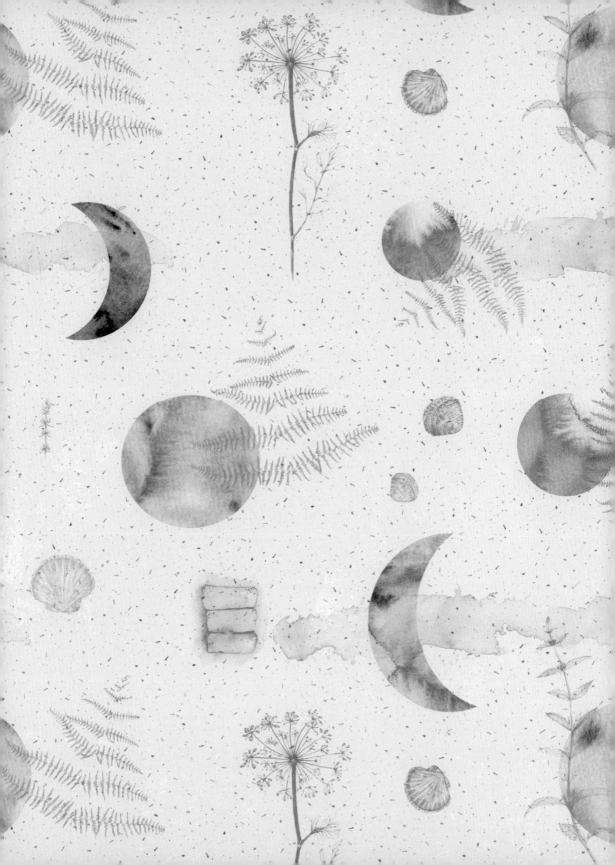